AF264759

The "Democratic Soldier": Comparing Concepts and Practices in Europe

---

Published by
Ubiquity Press Ltd.
6 Osborn Street, Unit 2N
London E1 6TD

Editors: Alan Bryden & Heiner Hänggi
Production: Yury Korobovsky
Copy editor: Cherry Ekins

This book was originally published by the Geneva Centre for the Democratic Control of Armed Forces (DCAF), an international foundation whose mission is to assist the international community in pursuing good governance and reform of the security sector. The title transferred to Ubiquity Press when the series moved to an open access platform. The full text of this book was peer reviewed according to the original publisher's policy at the time. The original ISBN for this title was 978-92-9222-284-0.

SSR Papers is a flagship DCAF publication series intended to contribute innovative thinking on important themes and approaches relating to security sector reform (SSR) in the broader context of security sector governance (SSG). Papers provide original and provocative analysis on topics that are directly linked to the challenges of a governance-driven security sector reform agenda. SSR Papers are intended for researchers, policy-makers and practitioners involved in this field.

The views expressed are those of the author(s) alone and do not in any way reflect the views of the institutions referred to or represented within this paper.

Suggested citation:
Mannitz, S. 2018. *The "Democratic Soldier": Comparing Concepts and Practices in Europe.* London: Ubiquity Press.
DOI: https://doi.org/10.5334/bbt. License: CC-BY 4.0

Contents

INTRODUCTION[1]

The new puzzle of democratic civil-military relations

The post-Cold War security environment, including the prevalence of unconventional security risks and an increase of armed conflicts within state borders, has created fundamental changes in the nature of democratic civil-military relations and security sector governance more broadly. Democratic governments now call more and more upon the armed forces to fulfil somewhat fuzzy tasks – partly civilian, partly humanitarian, partly military – in complex multinational missions and beyond the traditional rationale of defence, not least in domestic affairs.[2] In many countries military structures have been transformed for these new types of deployments, which fall both geographically out of area and thematically outside conventional defence imperatives. In view of the tremendous changes that have been wrought, it is astonishing that public attention and political debate on the possible implications of these new types of military missions have remained so limited in most of the countries concerned. This paper argues that this disconnect between new political practices and democratic contestation is both a result and an expression of the increased complexity of internal and external factors influencing how democracies shape their security policies and the institutions of their security sectors,[3] among which the military still occupies a prominent place.

From a theoretical perspective, all democracies are confronted with the same problem of having to deal with the tensions between the functional imperatives of military resources and the norms of their constitutional order, which prioritize non-violent solutions to conflicts. Democracies have to ensure this dilemma is resolved in such a way that the political system remains intact, regardless of whether the armed forces are only supposed to defend their country against external dangers, or lend weight to regional or global agendas, or also cooperate with other armies to implement UN resolutions. This implies that the armed forces must fulfil the tasks set down by a democratic government within a framework of control provisions that prevent possible military interventionism in politics and also any political misuse of the military by the executive.

There has never been a single fail-safe solution to this dilemma of democratic political control, nor do democratic states adhere to a single model or ideal type in this respect. The fact that democratic control arrangements have always differed from country to country complicates efforts by new democracies to reproduce similar control systems in the post-Cold War context. As a result, a new demand emerged for political advice and assistance in matters pertaining to the development of the security sector, reflected in the concept of security sector reform (SSR).[4] However, present-day conditions of globalized politics pose new challenges to current approaches to institution building and reform relating specifically to two key dimensions: increased uncertainty and changed perceptions.

The first major problem, increased uncertainty, arises from the fact that the principal challenge of democratic control of the military is different for a country still in the midst of democratization compared to a consolidated democracy. In the process of transformation, particular efforts need to be made to bind the armed forces to the new order. They must not exert undue influence on society and politics, or be used in violent attempts to (re)impose non-democratic rule. Societies undergoing democratization can look to consolidated democratic states for advice. However, there are significant differences between older democracies with regard to the role of the military, the activities in which the armed forces are authorized to engage and the ways in which democratic control is exercised in practice. In addition, previous democratization processes were framed by the Westphalian concept of bounded nation-states and thus countries developed their own forms of democratic rule within their own borders, without facing the same degree of influence from international interrelations and organizations as states democratizing in the post-Cold War era.[5]

The second major problem is that there have been fundamental changes in security perceptions and policies in the Western world, with corresponding waves of reforms and structural, strategic and operational transformations. These changed perceptions now shape contemporary democratic relations with military institutions. The new puzzle of democratic civil-military relations is particularly visible in Europe since the 1990s: the breakdown of the Soviet Union and its satellite states in Central, Eastern and Southeastern Europe left the successor states with the task of formulating a security policy based on new principles while also establishing a bond of loyalty between their armed forces and their young democratic systems. Many turned to NATO and the European Union (EU) in the search for new certainty, yet at the same time the changed global constellation prompted these Western organizations to rethink their conflict and risk scenarios. This triggered the replacement of conventional national defence doctrines with expanded concepts covering a much broader definition of security and what threats to it may entail.[6] Moreover, alliance structures have changed as a consequence of NATO's conceptual reinvention and enlargement; thus here, too, the armed forces have undergone a host of changes in their roles and functions. The question then arises of how these ongoing transformations in the defence sector of European democracies affect the domestic relations between the armed forces and wider society: how have the relationships between citizen, soldier and state changed?

The "democratic soldier": Still a relevant model?

The research presented in this paper is inspired by democratic peace theory and assumptions suggesting that security sector governance within democratic polities, especially civil-military relations, is characterized by specific qualities. The basic idea, originally put forward by the philosopher Immanuel Kant in his essay on perpetual peace,[7] claims that a democracy is the most peace-inclined type of regime because the power of the citizenry reduces the readiness of democratic states to make use of their military forces. Because of their interest calculations and basic value orientations, the people would risk neither their own health, lives and commonwealth nor those of their "own" soldiers, except in the case of ultimate necessity, i.e. self-defence.[8] This assumption implies that distinctive features and constraints characterize the relationship between citizens and their collective means of violence in a democracy. Both civilians and soldiers are understood to be loyal stakeholders in the polity, and their relationship is thus construed theoretically as one of mutual responsibility. But to what extent, if at all, does this hold true?

To shed light on the domestic relations between democratic societies and their armed forces, we can look at the impact the end of the Cold War and its resulting defence policy changes have had on civil-military relations in democratic states across Europe from a particular angle: how are the normative images and concepts of the ideal soldier (re)constructed in Europe today? Democratic peace theory suggests that democratic rule implies particularly responsible attitudes and behaviour when it comes to the use of force, while the main rationale of military reforms in European democracies in the past 20 years can be summarized as the increase of military efficiency, functionality and deployment capabilities. A first question is thus what do these reforms imply for the supposed bonds between the democratic citizenry and the military? Evoking the importance of a "subject perspective"[9] in civil-military relations, a second question asks what the current concepts of soldiering mean for individual members of the armed forces, their professional norms and their self-image.

For some time critics of existing research have demanded that more attention be paid to the "subject perspective" in civil-military relations,[10] but as yet the interplay between normative discourses on soldiering and institutional factors in democratic control of the military has remained comparatively underexplored.[11] Thus instead of describing how democratic control of the armed forces is organized institutionally in different countries, this paper focuses on the military as a social institution, faced with the task of translating the polity's (changing) normative concepts of the good democratic soldier into a meaningful agenda for the socialization of military personnel. In short, the aim is to scrutinize the practical relevance of the theoretical hypothesis that it is the ideal model of the "democratic soldier" which gives the armed forces in a democracy their "sense and purpose, structure and function".[12]

Following this introduction, the first section of the paper discusses the main considerations that inspired the study of democratic civil-military relations in this sample of European cases. It explains the failure of traditional approaches to democratic control of the armed forces in accounting for challenges in democratic civil-military relations after the end of the Cold War, and introduces democratic peace theory as an alternative approach to this theoretical impasse. The section ends by briefly describing the research design, which is based on in-depth, comparative studies of 12 European countries, conducted from 2006 to 2010 by a team of 16 scholars of ten nationalities.[13]

The second section presents the findings of the study, analysing common trends across Europe that have emerged in the transformation of the military into a multifunctional organization of security provision in a new democratic context. These trends are considered in light of the challenges of balancing military efficiency and the pressures of professionalization against the need to contain the risk of alienation between civilian society and the military and ensure the military is fully integrated within democracy. The official vision of the ideal-type national military force and the ways in which members of the armed forces understand their assigned roles and tasks are compared to assess the extent to which the democratic soldier remains an influential normative model and the degree of convergence among European democracies. The gap that unfolds between these two dimensions points to a number of practical dilemmas, notably in the area of military training, education and leadership.

The concluding section summarizes the main points of the research and comments on how these changes may affect a functioning culture of democratic control. It focuses particularly on the context specificity of the "democratic soldier" and other normative concepts meant to align the conduct of personnel in the armed forces with the wider values of the polity.

CIVIL-MILITARY RELATIONS IN EUROPEAN DEMOCRACIES

The end of the Cold War triggered significant changes in the way states on both East and West sides of the conflict conceptualized their domestic and external security. These changes led to new approaches to security sector governance that had especially profound consequences for the military and its place within European democracies. This section explains how the end of the Cold War set off several waves of defence reform, and why existing approaches to civil-military relations have proven limited in accounting for these new dynamics.

The military in European democracies after the end of the Cold War

On both sides of the former Iron Curtain the end of the Cold War washed away a number of certainties that had for nearly 50 years informed defence strategies and doctrines as well as conceptualizations of the enemy and possible military missions. This created an awkward vacuum in orientation for the armed forces in particular, as they had traditionally been accustomed to thinking in terms of the polarized patterns of great-power blocs and had derived their legitimacy and mission from this geostrategic confrontation.[14] Consequently, although the points of departure and the prospects for change differed between post-socialist countries and the former Western community, military institutions across Europe – and to a certain degree also in the United States – were forced to question their structural and conceptual organization and even the rationale of their future existence. NATO had lost its *raison d'être* as a collective system of defence,[15] and across Europe citizens asked for a so-called "peace dividend" in the form of a reallocation of public resources in favour of provision of social services or a tax reduction. In Switzerland citizens' initiatives called for the dissolution of the armed forces.[16] Although neither NATO nor the Swiss armed forces were dissolved, these two examples illustrate the broad scope of potential options that the breakdown of the Warsaw Pact made possible.

The collapse of the socialist world that started in 1989/1990 did in fact trigger what can be characterized as an era of continuous transformation and reform, of redefinition of roles and functions, and of structural reorganization of the military forces:[17]

> The end of the Cold War removed the spectre of a major European land war between east and west, and this had a direct impact on the principal role of armed forces; this has impacted on the centrality of the military mission of defence of national (and alliance) territory, towards other missions, notably military-to-military cooperation, peacekeeping and other "humanitarian" international operations ... Force structures have therefore been rapidly reduced in size, but within the context of less resources being made available, with the dual mantra, of the last decade and a half, of the aspiration to have "smaller but better forces".[18]

The end of the East-West confrontation and the reality of a diminished military threat thus made space for new considerations about the possible functions of the armed forces, leading to the embrace of new mission types and the adaptation of the structure of the armed forces to match these new roles. The redefinition of the military task spectrum during the 1990s in the NATO and EU areas took parallel paths in most European countries. In concrete terms this entailed several waves of defence reforms, which Karl Haltiner and Paul Klein[19] identified as three distinct phases.

- The downsizing wave, 1990–1995: aiming primarily to reduce manpower in order to lower costs and actualize the "peace dividend".
- The NATO-oriented wave of internationalism and professionalization, 1996–2000/2001: conceptual and strategic transformations of

> personnel recruitment to meet NATO standards for multinational troop deployment and achieve interoperability in new missions of a constabulary character.
>
> - The wave of modularization and "flexibilization", 2000/2001: accelerated downsizing as a result of restructuring to meet the goals of defence strategies that had now become transnational in character.[20]

One characteristic of the post-Cold War defence reforms becomes visible in the second and third waves in particular: they were conceptualized and implemented in close collaboration between the nation-states concerned and international actors, especially NATO and the EU. Seeking a new post-Cold War role, NATO reinvented itself in the 1990s, becoming a catalyst in reform processes as a "democratic and liberal transatlantic security community"[21] with a new operational scope. NATO opened up for enlargement, extended its activities and reformed its internal structures to enhance efficiency and allow for the creation of a political identity for collective security and defence based on shared values and norms. The latter is expressed particularly clearly in the Partnership for Peace programme (PfP) that NATO created in 1993 to foster dialogue across the former East-West divide and intensify inter-military cooperation in new domains, such as peacekeeping and humanitarian missions.[22] This outreach strategy to Central and Eastern Europe made the alliance a crucial agent of change. It also went hand in hand with EU efforts that, in the context of developing the European Security and Defence Policy, similarly redefined the scope of military tasks and capacity for expeditionary warfare to embrace humanitarian, peacekeeping and crisis management missions and "peacemaking".[23]

The result of NATO's involvement in these processes is, firstly, that "NATO standards have become the benchmark for the new profile of most of the European military organisations".[24] Secondly, the close interaction between national and international governance levels has had strong accelerating effects on defence reforms so that, in spite of the very different points of departure, already "16 years after the fall of the Berlin Wall the rapid progress of institutional reforms in many post-socialist states is leading to a convergence of concerns between west and central and eastern European states".[25] The speed of these processes is quite remarkable in view of the fundamental restructuring which the democratization of the political system and the demobilization of a huge and politicized military apparatus required in each case. It is even more so considering the particular challenges of staffing new political bodies and control organs in countries where all issues pertaining to the security sector in general and the armed forces in particular had been closely tied to the rule of the Communist Party and its members.[26]

The post-Cold War defence reforms, the end of mass armies and the appearance of new strategic discourses such as "world domestic policy", which frame unconventional new mission types, have been widely documented and analysed.[27] Yet less attention has been paid to the consequences of these changes for the model of democratic soldiering and the place of the soldier in democratic society and statehood.

The traditional notion of defence drew upon identification with the democratic polity, with the polity's "own" national sovereignty, history, territory and traditions; in other words, with the nation's imagery of communion to ensure mutual commitment and concern between civilians and the military.[28] From the perspective of members of the armed forces, the national collective, with its regime type and territory, is what was usually to be defended against external aggressors. Yet the contemporary realities of European soldiering do not reflect this scenario any longer. Seen from the perspective of members of the armed forces, the post-Cold War shift in security policies implies various challenges and pressures to adapt. Not only has the demand for qualifications grown as a result of the broadened mission scope (and the technological revolution in military affairs[29]), but new mission types, both geographically out of area and outside the imperatives of conventional national defence, also create a need to adopt a new image, develop new loyalties and adhere to different ethical foundations of soldiering than in the past. Where formerly the military served as nation builder and defender, what soldiers are now partly called upon to defend is more a set of transnational values rather than a bounded national collective, let alone territory.[30] This shift requires soldiers to cultivate a different professional identity than in the past and affects their domestic positioning in the relationship with civilian society and politics. As a result of these developments, traditional approaches to democratic civil-military relations seem to be of limited use when it comes to assessing the implications of contemporary (extended) security concepts and mission scopes for democratic soldiering, as discussed in the next subsection.

Traditional approaches to studying the military in democracy

The tradition of empirical research on democratic civil-military relations began in the late 1940s with the publication of *The American Soldier*, as part of a larger work on military social psychology in the Second World War.[31] The authors of this study were the first scholars to examine the concrete experiences, attitudes, motivations, rationales for action and behaviour patterns of soldiers. They investigated the processes by which individuals adapted to the military life-world and the way they dealt with their experiences of war. The study laid the foundations of military sociology as a field, which then developed a dual focus on the social psychology of the soldier and the organizational sociology of the military.[32] Quite apart from its relevance as the first major work of military sociology, this study contributed to reflection on social scientific methods by using the micro-perspective of American soldiers who had been involved in hostilities to develop an analysis of the macro-level foreign policy and events of the Second World War period. This approach pays tribute to the democratic promise, which understands the relationship between the citizenry and the armed forces as one of mutual responsibility and care. Observers of subsequent developments in this field have noted that empirical social research on the military since the 1950s reflects three main approaches.[33]

- *The social psychology of the soldier:* covering questions of cohesion, motivation, readiness for action and ways of coping with fear and stress in the military field of action, especially in small groups.
- *The organizational sociology of the military:* dealing with questions of hierarchy and leadership, organizational adaptation to technological challenges and the social consequences of the technological mechanization of the armed forces.
- *Analyses of the relation between the military and politics:* covering questions of oversight and institutional means of containing the risk of possible military coups.

With regards to the analysis of the relation between the military and politics, Günther Wachtler comments that this was usually done in a "purely descriptive way", frequently amounting to no more than a "formalistic way of looking at the issue".[34] Only rarely have systematic connections been made with more ambitious theoretical concepts of democratic control, leading Franz Kernic to state that social scientific research on the military in democracy "blatantly fails to offer any comprehensive, social-theoretical or critical perspective on the interrelation between society, politics, war, and military force".[35]

This disconnect between theoretical concepts of democratic control and social context is evident even in the debate about if and how the military may best be built in the context of democratic rule, which is by far the most prominent and longest-lasting debate within research on civil-military relations. Indeed, the question of if and how the military may best coexist with democratic rule has been marked by a rather narrow concentration on the parameters of professionalism and the functions of organizational structure. The two works that launched this controversy were Samuel Huntington's *The Soldier and the State* (1957) and Morris Janowitz's *The Professional Soldier* ([1960] 1971).[36] These books discussed the factual trend towards military specialization both in terms of technology and with reference to changes in the profile of standards for recruitment, training, the understanding of the soldier's role and the internal structure of modern armies. Huntington and Janowitz were in agreement about the main driving element in this transformation: the effects of rationalization and technological progress on the profile of qualifications required in the military. In his foreword to the 1971 edition of *The Professional Soldier*, Janowitz argued that the two world wars had effectively blurred the distinction between civilian and military affairs:

> It became appropriate to speak of the "civilianization" of the military profession and of the parallel penetration of military forms into civilian social structure ... In varying degrees, in most industrialized nations ... the new trend was toward smaller, fully professional, and more fully alerted and self-contained military forces.[37]

Although Huntington and Janowitz differed in their assessments of whether the supposed "civilianization of the military" was to be welcomed – Janowitz was pro and favoured a societal integration, while Huntington was against and argued for a social separation of the military – the way they focused their argument did much to influence subsequent debates. Civilian control of the military and the military's social position came mainly to be seen from an organizational perspective, typically focusing on the military structure. This focus relies on normative assumptions related to the theory of democracy, but it does not adequately incorporate this dimension into the argument. When the issue of democratic control gained new importance after the end of the Cold War, Peter Feaver pointed to this curious blank spot, which basically means that an abundance of findings exist on individual aspects yet no theoretical framework has been developed over the decades to guide the study of democratic civil-military relations:

> Neither [Huntington nor Janowitz] offers an adequate treatment of the civil-military problematique ... Both focus heavily on ... internal mechanisms for civilian control, values or professionalism variously specified, while slighting the external measures of traditional administrative theory ... A comprehensive theory of ... civilian control must also incorporate interest-based and external control mechanisms and, from a theoretical and a policy perspective, these deserve special emphasis.[38]

Not too surprisingly, there is broad agreement that in a democracy the military must respect the democratically legitimized political authority's right to issue directives, and obey them. After all, effective democratic control of the means of military violence is the standard precondition of a functioning democracy, and it is for this reason that establishing democratic civilian control of military power is absolutely vital in democratization processes. If one looks at the world of democratic states, however, one notices that there are considerable variations in the way even mature democracies shape their internal relations with their military institutions. Evidently, opinions differ about how strictly the principle of the subordination of the military to civilian political leadership must be interpreted in order to fulfil the requirement that civilian control should enjoy priority. To date, only a few monographs attempt a methodical treatment of the military as an institution embedded in democracy in different ways in different countries.[39]

This variance in approaches to democratic, civilian control of the military is apt to undermine established postulates: Huntington repeatedly stressed that his criterion of "objective control" consisted of a clear subordination of the military to the political leadership, and yet recent studies show that interpenetration between political and military levels in the political practice of mature democracies can exist without impairing democratic constitutional order.[40] There is just as much debate about whether such interpenetrations would contribute to overcoming what has been termed the "civil-military gap" as there is about the question of whether greater civil-military convergence would really be desirable. Some experts argue strongly (in the same vein as Samuel Huntington) that an army can only carry out its allotted tasks when the values determining its actions differ from the values of civilian life, on the grounds that "the existence of differences between a social group or a specific profession and society as a whole is not necessarily dysfunctional. All differences between the military and the society are not bad, and not all similarities are functional."[41] According to this view, it is precisely the functionality of the "civil-military gap" that accounts for the problematique of democratic civil-military relations, i.e. the normative dissonance with civilian society: soldiers are required to be prepared to use lethal military force and be able to wage war; but in the frame of democratic rule, they have to adhere to the clear normative preference for civil means of conflict resolution as well.[42]

A further limitation of the traditional preoccupation with institutional regulations stems from the observation that the primacy of civilian authority is frequently limited in the analysis to the political executive. Yet this approach seems increasingly inadequate as a way of steering democratic civil-military relations, because of the enormous complexity of societal, political, economic and media interrelationships in contemporary democracies. It has for that reason been argued in recent years that one can only speak of truly democratic control of the armed forces when more comprehensive democratic "governance" of the entire security sector has been attained. Such governance of the sector means that all state security services, including but not limited to the military, would be managed and held accountable to civilian democratic authority through several layers of institutional control and oversight provided by the legislature, the judiciary, independent statutory oversight authorities and wider civil society, including the media.[43] Some authors consider that important minimal indicators of this type of democratic control of the military could begin with at least the legislative branch enjoying the right to have a say in all matters pertaining to troop deployment,[44] as well as provisions for participation by citizens and the media in controversial decisions.[45] These criteria are more important than they have ever been, precisely because of the changes in world politics that have taken place since the end of the East-West conflict.

Civil-military relations are today subject to fundamentally different conditions, so existing literature cannot answer the question of which forms of integration of the military in democratic polities might be appropriate now or in the future. The significance of political culture and of changes in societal perceptions of the military is rarely addressed, and the research on the social processes beyond institutional reform in the civil-military relationship is particularly weak. In short, there are gaps in our knowledge of how institutional regulations, normative models and social practices, both in society and in the military, relate to one another, and how the rising level of international and transnational cooperation in foreign and security policy impacts on these relations.

The altered conditions of international politics suggest the usefulness of approaches addressing the different forms relations between society and the military may take within democracies.[46] While research on transition processes has looked more at the ways in which international organizations and military alliances influence reforms of post-socialist armed forces,[47] this literature has in general concentrated very much on the practical aspects of transition-related reform in the security sector and civil-military relations in post-socialist states: for example, the question of how the political system can be given the necessary capacities to establish an appropriate degree of control over the reformed armed forces has been examined in a number of individual studies that identify problems in dealing with legacies of the socialist era.[48] In contrast, there has so far been relatively little scholarly examination of the effects of intensified international and supranational security cooperation on security sector governance *within* states that cooperate, and in particular how these effects may play out between the military and the democratic sovereign. Little comparative research has asked how young democracies deal with the multiple pressures for reform that result not just from democratization, but also from the pressures of the simultaneous depoliticization and professionalization of their armed forces.[49]

In sum, insufficient attention has been paid to the subjective dimension of democratic political culture and its capacity for transformation because of a tendency in research and policy advice on security sector governance in general, and civil-military relations especially, to concentrate on aspects of organizational change and institution building. While proper institution building is essential, the democratization of formerly authoritarian systems also demands considerable societal readjustments. For example, one conspicuous aspect of this challenge is the fact that the formerly strained relations within society between civilians and soldiers must be transformed into a relationship of mutual trust. This kind of transformation cannot be brought about overnight and institutional innovations alone will not suffice. This is not only a problem in post-socialist states. The consolidated democracies of the West and their soldiers must also change their attitudes and collective identifications in circumstances where the agenda calls for cooperation in security policy, and in some cases even institutional integration between states which formerly belonged to opposing blocs. Given the poverty of conventional approaches to civil-military relations in accounting for the dilemmas of change currently faced by European democracies, democratic peace theory offers an innovative perspective, which the following subsection describes.

The democratic peace argument and democratic civil-military relations

From the perspective of research on civil-military relations, the theory of democratic peace is a promising, if unconventional, approach to explaining change in the relationship between the military, the citizen and the state in Europe's post-Cold War democracies. Democratic peace theory makes it possible to investigate relations within the state at the same time as examining the international dimension, and also has the potential to lead to insights relevant to theories of democratic rule. This is possible because although democratic peace theory refers primarily to the foreign policy behaviour of states, it also involves assumptions about the internal constitutional order of democracies.

In his treatise on peace, Immanuel Kant developed his theory of democratic peace to explain the foreign policy behaviour of democratic states and the driving forces behind such behaviour: in so doing, he also put forward a number of propositions about the position of the military in a democracy. He considered standing armies to create a problematic distance between citizens and the military apparatus, arguing instead for a citizens' army. As an army of defence, such an army could help realize the citizens' true inclination towards peace and assure the integration of the armed forces into the democratic system.[50] However, not all democracies fulfil this idealistic vision. Recent democratic peace research concerned with the drastic differences between democracies in participation in militarized inter-state disputes points to the strong influence of national political cultures on approaches to war and peace.[51] This puzzle of "democratic peace" *and* "democratic war" may find an explanation in the particular ways in which democracies deal with the means of military violence, depending on their citizens' attitudes towards the military and on how (much) democratic control of that institution is not only foreseen institutionally but also actually practised. Furthermore, it is possible to conclude that democratic citizenries develop a relationship to their soldiers that differs generally in quality from the relationship developed by their non-democratic counterparts, but that this relationship also shows path-dependent national idiosyncrasies.

Democratic control of the armed forces requires more than institutional structures to steer the military power apparatus and give military operations democratic legitimacy. The qualitative particularity of democratic states is the principle that the definition of the *volonté générale*, and hence also of the tasks entrusted to the military, should be developed in a process of deliberative negotiation. The actual fluidity and/or limitation of this process is subject to specific elements that arise as a result of the institutional order, the history of a country, its political culture and additional factors related to the specific conditions of democratic development. This suggests that focusing research on a normative model that is socially constructed in each case of democratic control will yield useful insights into the features of what is specifically democratic about these instances of civil-military relations. Following Immanuel Kant, one may state as follows: the democratically generated model of the armed forces, and those serving in them, has to reconcile the citizens' preference for the lowest possible level of material and personal expenditures with the necessity of, on the one hand, carrying out the defence functions and, on the other hand, satisfying the requirements of the international surroundings (both of which can vary). The normative concepts that govern the relationship between the military, the citizen and the state serve as a store of knowledge and foundation for communication over the role of the armed forces in a democracy. Based on this understanding, two dimensions of the normative aspects of civil-military relations in a democracy are to be distinguished analytically:

- the societal production of a normative model of the democratically controlled military and those serving in it; in other words the ideal of the "good soldier" in each democracy
- the conversion of these norms into structured socialization processes within military institutions, the results of which are expressed at the level of the individual soldier.

These two dimensions interact in the (re)production of soldiering concepts and their translation from normative models to an institutional culture. In every country soldiers pass through a socialization process which, in the ideal case, corresponds to the model of the democratic citizenry, and which influences a number of aspects: the relationship of those serving in the military to the primacy of political decision-making in general, and to the legitimate use of the military apparatus for certain operations and mandates in particular; the soldier's perception of international relations in general, and the distinction between friends and enemies in particular, etc. For example, if political neutrality is a marker of identity in the national political culture, one would expect to find this feature reflected in the normative image of the country's soldiers and their own conceptions of their role. In this way, the study of the ideal-type and real-type images of soldiering reflects the essential theoretical precepts of democratic peace research.

Finally, one should note that the theory of democratic peace names two further specificities of democratic states: interdependence and international organizations.[52] These factors explain the relative peaceableness of democracies by their fundamental preparedness to enter into mutual dependencies: democratic states are (more) willing to cooperate and also (more) capable of doing so when compared to non-democratic states. Cooperation, especially in defence alliances, requires that states adapt to the demands of closer functional and organizational integration. Cooperation and integration have gained increased importance in the past two decades as technological progress and post-Cold War changes in threat scenarios have together challenged conventional national defence objectives. Membership of international organizations also leads to a redefinition of military profiles: for example, through requests that forces be made available to support UN missions or pressure from the EU to meet certain conditions of membership. As a result, the range of tasks performed by many militaries has increased to such an extent that the original arguments in favour of armies of conscripts have reached their limits. Currently, professional volunteer armies have proliferated as a result, running contrary to Kant's proposition that a conscript militia system can resolve the dilemma of democratic control and defence capability. Certainly, conscription has never been the only recruitment system of democratic states, and over the past 20 years the majority of democratic states have established armies of contracted volunteers, *inter alia* in the hope of enhancing their forces' efficiency.

This shift towards volunteer forces entails possible problematic consequences for civil-military relations within democratic societies. It seems the political goal of performing as a good member of the international community has gained priority over arguments in favour of the democratic integration of the armed forces. Yet even under these changed circumstances, the crucial question remains of whether, and how, loyal relations are established between the military and democratic society on a domestic level. Moreover, volunteer forces raise questions concerning equity in burden sharing because the choice of contracted soldiers alters the fundamental position of military service towards citizenship and emphasizes the instrumental character of the armed forces. Since these aspects are central to the democratic governance of the military, applying democratic peace theory offers promising insight into civil-military relations and security sector governance more broadly, as discussed in more detail below.

To investigate the relevance of normative models for state, society and military relations in European democracies, the work at hand uses a comparative case study method, looking in detail at the features of civil-military relations and the broader context of security sector governance in 12 European countries. The research was conducted from 2006 to 2010 by a team of 16 scholars from ten countries. The following briefly describes some of the key theoretical and methodological elements of the research design, before moving on to discuss the findings of the comparison in the next section.

Research design: Normative models for the "democratic soldier"

Applying the lens of democratic peace theory to the central question of how European democracies manage the relationship between the military and society in the complex new security context of the post-Cold War era makes the focal point of this research the normative model that drives the socialization objectives of military institutions: this model is expressed in the "image of the democratic soldier". The normative model may be shaped by a range of possible factors in each specific case. For example, is the model marked by an emphasis on civil-military differences, so the military is expected to cultivate its uniqueness and separation from the civilian sphere? Or should the armed forces resemble civilian institutions as much as possible? Would the constituency's ideal be fulfilled if members of the armed forces saw themselves primarily as equal citizens who provide a particular service for the common good? Or would it rather be appreciated if the country's troops identified more with heroic archetypes of the warrior? Does the ideal-type soldier still have to be male, heterosexual and a member of the societal majority, or is the concept marked by openness to the existing societal diversity of the citizenry? Moreover, the relation between citizenship and military service may follow different patterns in different times and places: this is especially visible in decisions on the outsourcing of certain formerly military duties to either civilian services or private military companies.

Our research interest in the *different* ways in which democracies solve the problem of their ambivalent relationship to the military made it necessary to look not only at a number of cases but especially at cases that represent a certain degree of democratic variance. It can be assumed that the historical moment at which a country transitions to a democratic form of government shapes fundamental structures of its democratic culture (for example, through different democratic regime types), and this is highly likely to be reflected in both the preference for a certain type of military system and the normative model of the soldier reflected by the military.

Individual works point to such correlations between the moment and circumstances of a country's democratization and the institutional shape of that country's civil-military relations. For example, one study comparing the military constitutions of different European democracies suggests there is greater trust in the functioning of checks and balances to control the military in states with a long democratic tradition than in younger democracies, which take more extensive precautions to protect the newly established political order.[53] It is most likely that such particularities also influence the attitudes of citizens and soldiers towards one another. One can hence suspect that national conceptualizations of the ideal military, and public contestations over the features it may or may not bear, reflect domestic perceptions of legitimacy and security, both at the outset and as they change over time.

Yet both democratic and military-political cultures are influenced not only by the national histories of their specific context but also by the context of international relations in which they are embedded. In the European context, this concerns in particular the relationships states may have with international organizations (such as NATO and/or the EU), and political markers in the field of security (such as a state policy of political neutrality). Based on these considerations, it was important to look at cases from different historical phases of democratization and with different positions *vis-à-vis* the international community. Arranged according to the age and phase of their democratic systems, the countries selected as the case study sample are listed in Table 1.[54]

Post-socialist countries are overrepresented in the case sample in view of the importance of democratic control of the military during system transformation, and also because, even some years later, less is known

Table 1: Case study selection

Traditional democracies	United Kingdom, Switzerland
Consolidated democracies	Germany, Spain
Post-socialist democracies	Estonia, Lithuania, Poland, Romania, Serbia, Czech Republic, Hungary
In democratization	Ukraine

about domestic relations since regime change. At the same time, the inclusion of West European states, both traditional and consolidated in character, made it possible to assess the impact of democratic maturity. Table 2 provides an overview of the relevant key features of the countries studies, namely NATO/EU membership, type of recruitment, proportion of women and service restrictions for women in the armed forces.

The comparative analysis was based on analysis of written material and the contents of training and education curricula. It also draws on non-participant observation in military academies and semi-structured interviews with soldiers (mostly non-commissioned officers and officer ranks).[55]

The research is limited in its relevance by its exclusive focus on European contexts: although the interaction between local, domestic dynamics and larger international and transnational pressures for reform are also of interest to post-conflict contexts in particular, the results are of limited applicability. Further, the study of transnational dynamics of security policies and their possible domestic effects is not far advanced, thus the research is limited in the resources it can draw on with respect to this question. These limitations notwithstanding, the research does meet its goal of comparing the defence reform processes of a sample of countries facing similar security challenges. The results of this comparative analysis are presented in the next section.

Table 2: Overview of key features of the countries studied

	NATO Member-ship	Member of EU and its precursors	Type of recruitment	Proportion of women (as of)	Service restrictions for women
Traditional democracies					
Switzerland	No	No	Militia with conscript service and small proportion of professional soldiers (conscript ratio 89% as of 2010)	0.5% (2010)	No restrictions
United Kingdom	Yes	Yes; since 1973	Professional volunteer army	9.5% (2009)	No use in combat
Consolidated democracies					
Germany	Yes	Yes; since 1952	Volunteer army; general male conscription suspended since July 2011, but not abolished and still in force under constitutional law	8.9% (2009)	No restrictions
Spain	Yes	Yes; since 1986	Professional volunteer army (conscription ended in 2001)	18.3% (2009)	No restrictions
Post-socialist democracies					
Czech Republic	Yes	Yes; since 2004	Professional volunteer army (conscription formally ended in 2005)	13.4% (2011)	No restrictions
Estonia	Yes	Yes; since 2004	Conscript army, but with a militia-system military reserve (conscript ratio 39.5% in 2009)	9.5% (2009)	No restrictions
Hungary	Yes	Yes; since 2004	Professional volunteer army (conscription ended in 2005)	19.6% (2008)	No restrictions
Lithuania	Yes	Yes; since 2004	Professional volunteer army (conscription suspended in September 2008)	11.5% (2009)	No restrictions
Poland	Yes	Yes; since 2004	Professional volunteer army, conscription ended in 2008.	1.6% (2009)	No restrictions

Romania	Yes	Yes; since 2007	Professional volunteer army since 2007 (conscription formally ended in 2004)	6.4% (2006)	No restrictions
Serbia	No	No	Professional volunteer army (conscription ended 2011)	0.3% (2007)	No restrictions
In democratization					
Ukraine	No	No	Conscript army (conscript ratio: no data available)	13.0% (2009)	No restrictions

Sources: International Institute for Strategic Studies, *Military Balance 2011* (London: IISS, 2011); *Der neue Fischer-Weltalmanach: Zahlen, Daten, Fakten* (Frankfurt/M.: Fischer Taschenbuch Verlag, 2011); Global Defence homepage, www.globaldefence.net; NATO homepage, www.nato.int; Swiss Army extranet, www.extranet.vtg.admin.ch; Bundesheer homepage, www.bundesheer.at; Serbian armed forces homepage, www.vs.rs; Ukrainian armed forces homepage, www.mil.gov.ua.

THE "DEMOCRATIC SOLDIER" IN PRACTICE: CONVERGENCE AND VARIANCE

As described above, the new security context of the early 1990s began to change the way European countries conceived the role of their militaries. European countries which formerly belonged to hostile power blocs became partners interested in cooperation. New resources of collective identification and separation came into being. The East-West confrontation was replaced by a much more diffuse picture of possible conflict and threat scenarios, all of which challenge not only the traditional parameters of national defence but also the legitimating arguments for the maintenance of mass armies and/or conscription-based defence structures, and their related conceptualizations of soldiering. Newly defined security threats, whether transnational terrorism or the governance disasters created by dysfunctional states in other parts of the world, have nevertheless been answered with military operations. In the wake of such deployments, reforms were launched which changed both the structure and the functions of the armed forces in many countries across Europe to meet the altered requirements. A number of notable trends, reflecting these changes, emerged from the comparative analysis.

New concepts of the soldier in the post-Cold War era

The case comparison revealed a striking convergence among the European democracies in the sample towards professional, volunteer forces. This change has had several important implications for the normative model of soldiering within these militaries and their integration within their respective democracies. This section describes the demise of the image of the conscripted defender of the nation-state as a normative guideline for the European soldier.

There are single exceptions, and the degrees and the speed of the reforms differ, but on the whole the majority of European states – if they did not already have professional volunteer forces, like the UK – decided in the 1990s to maintain smaller armed forces and staff them no longer with conscripts but with contracted volunteers. In contrast to conscripts, these volunteers obtain high-level training to develop specialist expertise and become capable of collaborating with friendly foreign armies within the modular structures of collective defence systems and multinational missions.[56] In all the cases studied, the official concept of the appropriate soldier of today stresses the relevance of skilled specialist expertise, high motivation and discipline levels, and the ability to perform in complex international missions that require an outstanding level of social as well as military capability.

The convergence among cases at the level of the official discourse is overwhelming: over a decade after the end of the Cold War all but one of the post-socialist democracies under study had made a transition to a professional volunteer army, reflecting the same emphasis on professional volunteerism found in the traditional and consolidated democracies of Western Europe. The participation of women in the armed forces also appeared as a marker of normative convergence, with no service restrictions for women in any case bar the one exception of a restriction on service in combat in the UK. Moreover, the average proportion of women in the armed forces among the cases studied was approximately 10 per cent: outliers Spain and Hungary reached almost double this proportion with nearly 18.3 per cent and 19.6 per cent in service respectively. These changes in the nature of the military institution were made within the larger context of cooperation with, or preparation to join, NATO and the EU (only Serbia, Switzerland and Ukraine did not become members of both organizations during the 2000s). Table 3 brings further detail to the convergence of official discourse in normative models of professionalization, compiling relevant keywords from cases in an overview.

Table 3: Overview of keywords for national images of the soldier

Country	Attributes attached to soldiering in official discourse
Czech Republic	Citizen soldier: warrior to fight and defend country; professional for out-of-area missions and crisis management
Estonia	Professionalism, patriotism and respect; uniqueness, combining skills which cannot be obtained elsewhere
Germany	"Citizen in uniform", focusing on concept of the whole person: military expert and (non-partisan) politically educated soldier; responsible consciousness; freedom of thought; defence of freedom of German people
Hungary	Professionalism: patriotism, loyalty, courage, comradeship, respect, honesty, discipline
Lithuania	Soldier as a defender of the Motherland; soldier as a professional fighting battles in foreign lands
Poland	Professional expert in military technology; highest possible educational standards; education in the military shall enable cultural promotion of the individual and follow democratic standards
Romania	Professional military expertise and cultivation of general leadership skills and personality; double specialization for military graduates encompasses courses in leadership, management and sociology; fighter and branch specialists; responsible, knowledgeable about national and international culture, legislation, international human rights law; displays civilized behaviour

Serbia	Military expert with civilian soft skills; military tasks are deterrence, defence of Serbian territory and airspace, participation in international military cooperation and multinational operations, assistance to civilian authorities in countering internal security threats, separatism, organized crime and terrorism, and assistance in cases of natural or man-made catastrophes
Spain	Values connected with professional soldier: respect for superiors and subordinates, discipline, preparation (technical and physical), teamwork, enthusiasm for overcoming obstacles, capacity for organization, ability to command, collaboration, sense of duty, observance of obligations, loyalty, comradeship and exemplarity – professional behaviour as an example for society
Switzerland	Citizen soldier, combining military defence capabilities with civic values; developing skills for interoperability, teamwork and empathy; lawfulness of behaviour; relevance of international humanitarian law is stressed
UK	High-level professional, technologically advanced, apolitical forces; well-educated and trained individual who shows initiative and consideration; prepared to make sacrifices; lawful and appropriate behaviour, total professionalism; selfless commitment, respect for others, loyalty, integrity, discipline, courage; "force for good" in the world
Ukraine	Professionalism as attribute of ideal soldier and commander; faithful devotion to Ukrainian people; defence of Ukrainian territory, freedom, Ukrainian state and its independence

Sources: Keywords extracted from empirical country reports, www.hsfk.de/Das-Bild-vom-demokratischen-Soldaten-Spannungen-z.75.0.html?&L=1, and the joint publication of the research results: Sabine Mannitz (ed.), *Democratic Civil-Military Relations. Soldiering in 21st Century Europe* (London/New York: Routledge, 2012).

Two arguments for organizational efficiency explain the accelerated establishment of volunteer armies. To begin with, the latest developments in information and weapons technology, associated with the so-called "revolution in military affairs", require a level of training that conscripts would be unable to gain in the course of their basic military training. This reverberates with what Morris Janowitz, and later Charles Moskos, judged to be the unstoppable effect of technological development: the pressure towards specialization and functional differentiation. Advanced weapon systems need fewer and fewer personnel; but these personnel must be better qualified. However, it is not only organizational aspects of task-oriented management and more efficient use of resources that have undermined the rationale for compulsory military service; changes in military tasks themselves have also made longer-serving staff a necessity. In other words, the qualification profiles required for today's military tasks mean that the cost-benefit ratio of investments – which was among Kant's arguments for militia structures – has shifted away from conscript systems towards smaller vocational armies supported by (cheaper) civilian service providers; a type of armed forces Moskos calls the "postmodern military".[57] For NATO member states this shift is documented in the New Strategic Concept, which outlines an unconventional set of tasks for the alliance. The complexity of multinational missions, which has only increased in the post-Cold War milieu, adds further to qualification demands, especially training for and experience in inter-military and civil-military cooperation:

> NATO's New Strategic Concept, according to Article V of the Washington agreement, strengthens the coexistence of traditional Alliance defence and global missions that serve Alliance security, and, beyond that, further the goal of the implementation of NATO-defined values in the form of "humanitarian intervention" – in extreme cases the prevention of genocide. Both aims often end up converging – such as in the cases of Bosnia-Herzegovina, Kosovo and Afghanistan: NATO "puts its foot down" where its security interests are either directly or indirectly affected, and, concurrently, it spreads the liberal-democratic values that characterize the constitutions of its member states.[58]

The irrelevance of military missions to immediate national security has changed the traditional rationale for maintaining the military: in short, something that was once genuinely the defence institution of a nation-state has been developing into a multifunctional organization that is expected to be capable of performing a panoply of tasks for security provision in a rather wide sense, ranging from waging wars (with the help of technological equipment, which itself produces high demands and transformation pressures) to performing missions of humanitarian help, border control, policing, assisting reconstruction work, or even state building, such as in the case of Afghanistan. In a sense, military tasks have become less conventionally military, while formerly non-military tasks have become security concerns:

> Since the end of the Cold War, we have witnessed a substantive widening and deepening of the concept of security. On one hand, non-military security issues ... are now broadly accepted as component parts of a meaningful security agenda. Furthermore, military threats and the ways states respond to them have changed ... Asymmetrical threats and warfare, as well as the blurring of the lines between different dimensions of traditional and new security issues, have emerged as characteristic features.[59]

The political missions that have motivated European democracies to deploy their military forces since the 1990s reflect very clearly this paradigmatic change and expanded perception of security threats, which challenge the relations between society, the political executive and the armed forces in a democracy.[60] For these domestic relationships it makes a great difference whether soldiers are supposed to defend their country against an attack – i.e. wage a "war of necessity" – or whether a government sends the troops into a "war of choice" to achieve what is seen as being in the national interest (including providing for regional stability or conducting a humanitarian intervention).[61] Although the citizenry of each country may show different patterns of consent or dissent over such issues, democratic governments have to be able to justify their "wars of choice". Their common post-Cold War problem is that criteria for the legitimate deployment of the troops are much harder to determine in the face of blurry security risks. Consequently, it becomes increasingly difficult to define what soldiers are actually meant to be prepared for. Moreover, the less a military mission relates to a nation's defence, the more difficult it is to explain the reason for calling up that nation's conscripts. The latter dilemma is clearly reflected in the transformations that were initiated in countries with conscription systems like Germany, Switzerland and Serbia in response to their increased international commitments.

In sum, among the countries in our sample the typical democratic soldier is no longer depicted as the brave conscript who defends the nation-state, but rather as the well-trained professional, skilled manager and flexible expert who adjusts the choice of his or her instruments to the particularities of very different missions. It may be expected that countries which adhere to a different ideal are either politically neutral, more hesitant than others to participate in unconventional military missions, or stick to territorial defence doctrines. This proposition indeed appears to hold to some degree: Switzerland, Estonia and Ukraine are the only countries in the sample that continue to maintain their traditional conscription systems and hold most strongly to territorial defence. In these cases, the soldier is still stressed as being first and foremost a defender of the country, and only to a lesser extent part of a global "force for good". Serbia and Germany are two further examples where conscription was ended rather later than in other cases (in 2011). In Germany the post-Second World War obligation to have a defence-oriented military – which is also a principle anchored in the constitution – has created a military political culture based on a deep reservation about the use of arms. This reservation is slowly being replaced with legitimizing constructions, in which defence of Germany in a broad sense is made an argument for the deployment of troops to support UN, NATO or EU missions. Serbia's abolition of the draft had a different rationale: politically neutral, the country has been occupied with concerns about its territorial integrity, as the independence declaration of its former province of Kosovo in 2008 exemplifies. However, the costliness and comparative inefficiency of a conscript army, together with the pressure of EU preference for a smaller and more professional military suitable for international integration, finally put an end to the universal service obligation. Moreover, although Serbia keeps a low profile in international engagement, it does contribute to UN peacekeeping missions and is therefore in need of military professionals.[62]

These cases show that the question of whether a democratic state opts for an army of conscripts or a military of volunteers, or a combination of both systems, depends firstly on the particular state's historical experiences, and secondly on the priorities that dominate the setting at certain time points. In the post-Second World War Federal Republic of Germany, conscription was considered the best option by German military reformers as well as by the occupying countries and later allies. Their principal aim was to rearm the Western part of Germany while ensuring the democratic integration of the newly founded military to prevent relapses into German militarism and further democratize the young republic with the help of a civic education programme for the drafted recruits. The Bundeswehr concept of the "citizen in uniform" mirrors these aims, linking citizenship, military service and defence of the polity. Under the model of universal conscription, (male) citizens were thought to have not only the right but also the duty to use armed force to defend their polity. With the disappearance of territorial defence probabilities, this understanding of the soldier lost plausibility. In effect, the ways in which democracies staff their military systems have become much more similar over the past 30 years.

In the post-socialist cases of democratization, the entry conditions of international organizations like NATO and the EU, together with previous bad experiences of conscription as an instrument of party political indoctrination, prompted the majority of Europe's young democracies to decide in favour of a volunteer army right from the start. As in the West, reforms replaced conscription with all-volunteerism almost everywhere and were welcomed by the societies as a reflection of the desired "peace dividend". In their sum, today's central arguments speak against the draft, whereas concerns about the democratic or societal integration of armed forces that have always supported conscript systems have come to rank secondary. While these rationales are still the major argument for conscription in Switzerland, both Estonia and Ukraine have other reasons: they have not abolished conscription because of their geopolitical situation in the immediate neighbourhood of Russia. The extent of this convergence in European models of military integration in democracy raises the immediate question of the extent to which these democracies still have variance in their national models. Findings relevant to this question are presented next.

Continuity and change among European democracies

The demand for operational capability in complex missions around the globe appears to cut across the diversity of democratic states, and to a certain degree it does so foremost in respect of organizational structures. Also, quite surprisingly in view of the great differences between national political cultures, the model-type image of the contemporary soldier has become very similar. As mentioned, he or she is less and less defined by male warrior attributes and expectations of home defence, but increasingly characterized as an expert in military technology with a high level of very different, more general and civilian skills; someone who may be sent anywhere to achieve security policy aims in the frame of multinational missions that meet national criteria of legitimacy.

However, in their normative conceptualizations of the soldier the countries studied continue to express particular features, values and traditions. Thus in spite of the overall observable trend towards all-volunteer forces, democratic states still deal in different ways with the fundamental problem of how to establish a balance between democratic containment of the military and the latter's operational capabilities. Yet nowadays this variance centres more on other aspects rather than on the type of recruitment system. For example, aspects of differentiation are now the concrete forms of democratic control and deliberation over the sending of troops, the scope of military missions that are regarded as legitimate and, partly as a result of these different features, the situation of soldiers in democracy in terms of their rights, duties, tasks and professional loyalties.[63]

With the installation of vocational all-volunteer armies, the implementation of democratic control provisions has gained new relevance, for this recruitment system increases the potential roles of the armed forces.[64] The fear exists – among political observers as in some military circles – that inhibitions about deploying the military could recede if military service was primarily defined as a profession and based on voluntary choice.[65] To contain such dangers, all democracies have institutionalized checks and balances, even if these take considerably different forms. In some democracies, democratic control is considered to be sufficient if the armed forces are subject to the supreme command of an elected head of state, as for example in Hungary. Other democracies provide for an obligation to inform parliament or make decisions on (certain) military operations subject to approval by the legislature.[66] One such example is the German legislation that requires parliamentary participation in decisions on foreign deployment of the military. Democracies also continue to differ with regard to the agreed political mission of their armed forces. Whereas former colonial powers, such as Great Britain, have traditionally always deployed their military resources outside their own state territories to project their power and enforce their political interests abroad, other democratic states keep closer to the original concept of maintaining an army for national defence purposes and just a few types of international operations with a special mandate. This is the case in Switzerland, for example, where foreign engagement is limited to peacekeeping. Some democracies subordinate their defence doctrine to collective security systems like NATO and subscribe to their criteria for legitimate military operations, while other emphasize their basic defensive posture with a policy of neutrality, which in our sample is the case with Switzerland, Serbia and Ukraine.

There is a corresponding variety of concepts regarding the appropriate legal position of soldiers. Although they are all obliged to keep political orientation out of their service duties, there is wide variation in how far this is understood to reach, depending mostly on national historical experience. In Germany the democratic soldier possesses as many civil and political rights as possible, even when on duty, in order to be a "citizen in uniform" – a concept which applies to not only drafted conscripts but also longer-serving contracted soldiers.

The United Kingdom, Poland and Spain impose obligations of political neutrality on their soldiers, which limit their basic rights and also extend even beyond their terms of duty. In all these countries, members of the armed forces are not allowed to join political parties, as this is considered too political an activity.[67] Typically, it is these traditional elements in the various national concepts of the soldier which survive, in spite of the latest reforms and transformations designed to impart a new image of the soldier. In other words, the new concepts do not wash away the older ones, but are rather adopted as additions – and they create new tensions. The figure of the citizen soldier has been linked with conscription systems, but in countries like Germany and Switzerland, where the democratic soldier concept has relied on this tradition from the beginning, the ideal is neither suspended along with conscription (as in Germany) nor replaced by the new image of the career soldier (as in Switzerland).

In the post-socialist countries, the desire to maintain a distinct legacy of their own democratic history also features. But in many of these cases, what has been revitalized to represent the stock of national traditions stems less from the most recent phases of democratization than from the pre-socialist past and the (rather weak and nationalist) democratic states that existed in the interwar period. These inconsistent mixtures complicate the official present-day concept of the democratic soldier: thus, while post-modern arguments for "world domestic politics" and good international citizenship are regularly mobilized when it comes to legitimizing participation in foreign missions under UN or NATO mandates, the dominant national perceptions of soldiering still draw on the traditional concept of the patriotic defender of the home country.

These tensions in official concepts of the contemporary democratic soldier are typical expressions of simultaneous reforms which followed different rationales and responded to competing pressures from national electorates and international partners and organizations respectively. In the contemporary image, the soldier is actually meant to become

> a complex composite: a national asset perceived as an international representative, a professional fighter assumed to sport humanitarian values, and an individual accountable both to the law and to the hierarchy faced by opponents outside both. In short, this is an individual expected to maintain the external appearance and all the capabilities of the traditional soldier, though not too blatantly with regard to fighting on the streets, who is equally expected to have the capabilities and inclinations of a humanitarian operative. Furthermore, the militaries composed of these soldiers are taken to be an amalgamation of all these qualities, as understood in civilian terms.[68]

This set of expectations constructs a demanding hybrid[69] of civilian and military capabilities and thus confirms the above-quoted processes of "civilianization" and "constabularization" that Morris Janowitz foresaw in the 1960s.[70] Two typical examples may suffice to illustrate the ambivalence implied in these mixed images. In the Czech Republic, the official ideal can best be described as the citizen soldier who is a well-trained member of the military but also a representative of the spirit of Czech democracy. However, the military qualities identified as guiding norms in the Military Code are a mixed set of rather warrior-like features (honour, bravery, discipline, obedience, readiness for self-sacrifice, etc.) and more general professional virtues (sense of duty and responsibility, loyalty, honest and principled behaviour, etc.). Likewise, in Lithuania the members of the armed forces are to be technically competent and militarily skilled, yet at the same time committed to a definite system of values. They are in charge of territorial defence of the homeland, but also tasked to be a force for global and regional stability operations that defend the security, democracy and welfare of the country's NATO allies and EU member states, as well as freedom and democracy in the neighbouring regions of the EU.[71] The nature of hybrid civilian and military capabilities in the new roles of the military suggests that military institutions and soldiers individually must adapt to these changes: the extent of these efforts at adaptation are discussed below.

Selective adaptations: Soldiers' perceptions of their roles and tasks

Theoretically, the model of the "good soldier" projected in official documents and materializing in national defence structures is something that should correspond to the convictions of the democratic constituency and at the same time reflect that polity's specific requirements in defence policy. On the one hand, it is meant to be an expression of collective goals in defence and security, which the armed forces are expected to satisfy effectively. On the other hand, apparent contradictions between military effectiveness and democratic principles notwithstanding, the armed forces must form a trustworthy subsystem of the democratic system. These fundamentals create a tension that individual soldiers have to solve in their own understanding of their function, role and tasks as members of the armed forces in a democracy. Models of the soldier specific to each national context can therefore also be understood as representing a consensus proposal on how democratic principles and military imperatives might be reconciled in the given setting. Yet this solution to the dilemma is not necessarily convincing or satisfying for all the affected personnel.

Evidently, the impact of the transformation and the resulting pressures on soldiers to adapt vary in degree among different countries, depending on their previous definitions of the military's functions and national power projections. For example, the British armed forces were traditionally used in foreign deployments, and thus being reconceptualized in the post-Cold War world as military "forces for good" on a global scale is for them a minor change. In contrast, German Bundeswehr soldiers previously derived their tasks from the Cold War rationale of deterrence and a national, as well as alliance, defence scenario. Thus for German troops the change to being deployed in Sudan, Uganda, the Democratic Republic of the Congo or Afghanistan could hardly be greater. Certainly, those young people who have joined the Bundeswehr in recent years do so under these changed circumstances. Nevertheless, the older staff are expected to make these young people understand what they are trained and employed for, and many of these more experienced soldiers have their own difficulties in coping with the changed role of the military. Moreover, political decisions for or against the sending of troops have not always been clear enough on the relevant criteria, nor the mission goals. Such inconsistencies create identity confusion among soldiers in many of the countries studied,[72] but the problem is most pronounced in the post-socialist settings where no traditional image of the *democratic* soldier can ease the embrace of new tasks and identity aspects, but where patriotic service to the nation is a much stronger narrative than in the West European cases. This is also mirrored in the soldiers' individual perceptions of military roles and tasks.

To illustrate this dynamic, we turn again to the case of Lithuania, which has already been evoked as an example of how the old and the new normative models of the soldier become conflated: as mentioned, the Lithuanian soldier is understood as a defender of the motherland (conventional modern concept), and as a professional who fights battles in foreign lands (post-modern concept).[73] The post-modern concept of soldiering was layered on to the conventional modern concept as a result of Lithuania's membership in NATO and the EU. In this process, global templates and texts were integrated into strategic documents, thereby paying tribute to NATO's security concept. Yet the new additions to the model do not seem to be convincing on the ground: when asked for their own ideas of soldiering, the motivations of their professional choice and the rationale of the armed forces more generally, soldiers in Lithuania referred firstly to devotion and love for their homeland and the Lithuanian army.

The more abstract vision of defence of collective values was hardly mentioned.

A second example of the same tensions in the post-Cold War adaptation of the model of soldiering comes from the Czech Republic, where a democratic citizen soldier concept had developed early in the twentieth century. In the post-Cold War era much trust seems to be placed in public consciousness of the country's earlier democracies, even though this "democratic heritage" was lost in intervening decades and knowledge of the period cannot be taken for granted among today's younger generations. These conditions, together with the complete absence of related teaching content from the Czech armed forces' training curricula, create a situation where "the national tradition" is not known, let alone understood, among those who are meant to see themselves as citizen soldiers. The official concept, which is quite similar to the Lithuanian example, briefly holds that a Czech soldier has two functions: that of the warrior (fighting for defence of the country), and that of the specialist professional (serving in out-of-area missions and crisis management alongside other NATO forces). However, little is done in the training and education of soldiers to clarify how these two different images of the democratic soldier could be reconciled:[74] as a result, the soldiers interviewed insisted on the relevance of territorial defence as the central source of their professional identity, despite the fact that this vision stands in contradiction to the explicit security concept of the Czech Republic.

Interviews with soldiers in all countries studied revealed that the transformation of the international system and the diffusion of threats in the context of extended concepts of security have made it increasingly difficult for a great number of them to understand their professional missions. Apparently, in the military, national defence continues to be the most accepted mission goal, while unconventional expeditionary missions evoke mixed feelings. This dynamic relates to a second factor, namely a perceived lack of recognition.

Across our sample, an impressive number of soldiers expressed negative sentiments about the status of the military in public esteem, and this finding applies even in countries where opinion polls indicate very high appreciation of the armed forces. Soldiers miss social and political recognition of the military profession. While this may sound like a discourse of self-pity, it can in fact be explained by the imbalance created by the increased complexity and high risk inherent to new missions, and a concomitant lack – in the perception of the soldiers affected – of political explanation and/or public support. Although the attitudes of national societies towards the use of force differ, public discussions scrutinizing the legitimate scope of military action are rare. Many soldiers perceive this as a sign of the carelessness and alienation of their society and their government – in other words, as a sign of a deepening civil-military gap.

We further gained the impression from among the more senior officer ranks in particular that experienced soldiers are disappointed and feel left alone if missions are not clearly explained and if the people who are to exert democratic control of the military do not know much about military affairs; or if politicians do not differentiate clearly between the goals of civilian/humanitarian and military mission tasks. For these reasons, the idea that soldiering could be (merely) regarded as a profession meets with considerable uneasiness on the part of many experienced soldiers, who are justified in their demand that decisions regarding their deployment be made with consideration of constitutional values. This demonstrates that the tensions existing between old and new concepts of the soldier are not just ideational symbols of the rumblings that can arise between the armed forces, the government and democratic constituencies concerning questions of the legitimate mission of the military. Although the military is expected to respect the primacy of political decision-making and must not engage in politicking itself, being charged with "doing a good job" implies that it shall in practice support the political message of any given mission.

Christopher Dandeker has drawn attention to the fact that contemporary "wars of *contested* choice"[75] do not provide the armed forces with reliable political and public support for their missions. This may be interpreted as an expression of the weakening of traditional bonds between national societies and their armed forces under the influence of indirect notions of national defence. However, this tendency also points to the growing necessity of providing today's soldiers with adequate resources for the maintenance of psychological stability and scrutinizing the sense of what they are called upon to deliver. In other words, if soldiers are to learn to see themselves as defenders of a post-national value community, more than new requirements for the training agenda will be necessary. The dilemmas posed by these new contradictions between models, missions and perceptions are discussed below.

Dilemmas in contemporary training requirements

The assemblage of national defender figures with post-modern mission scopes in the official concepts of the soldier is marked by contradictions that also surface in the formulation of military leadership ideals and education goals. The extraterritorial intervention and crisis operations which democratic countries have supported in recent years imply that their soldiers are now performing duties ranging from military combat to tasks once the purview of civilian humanitarian aid organizations.[76] Moreover, the role of the military has also changed within the domestic context with respect to the fulfilment of politically motivated missions:

> The strategic use of force is exceptional as the military is asked to achieve political goals, and normally the most that can be expected is a condition in which an acceptable outcome can be delivered by the political process. In doing so, the military becomes engaged in a complex and interdependent political and military network with its government as it seeks to deliver that "condition", often in ways that require the management of different missions (for example, counterinsurgency and reconstruction in different or even the same areas of the theatre). At the same time, tensions between coalition participants need to be mitigated while relations with non-military actors also need to be managed.[77]

The complexity of the tasks mentioned here is most demanding. It comes as no surprise, then, that for military training and leadership education the expanded scope of possible military functions poses practical challenges. Even longer-serving volunteers, who obtain much more intensive training than previous generations of conscripts, are difficult to train in accordance with such numerous and heterogeneous demands. After all, soldiers are not only expected to integrate civilian skills, but must also be able to distinguish, at times within seconds, the best response to a given situation. Soldiers who are sent into complex missions – such as EUFOR RD Congo (European Union Force République Démocratique du Congo) in the Democratic Republic of the Congo and NATO Operation Enduring Freedom or ISAF (International Security Assistance Force) "peace enforcement" activities in Afghanistan – cannot simply act as if they were warriors because doing so would undermine their soft mission goals.

The consequences are reflected at the level of official declarations, and it is generally acknowledged that the training and education of military leaders must be adapted to the new environment of such international missions. In many cases civilian learning content, such as knowledge of international law, soft skills and training in intercultural competencies, is declared to be of growing importance, even though it is not necessarily integrated systematically into the military education scheme. While some very advanced training is given in special programmes, such as that offered by the International Association of Peacekeeping Training Centres (initiated by the Canadian Pearson Peacekeeping Center in 1995), not all soldiers sent into peacekeeping missions enjoy such a high standard of training beforehand; nor are the difficulties of growing complexity restricted to peacekeeping missions. Strong emphasis is, for that reason also, placed on soldiers' greater ownership in decision-making within the boundaries of commands. The ideal of decentralized leadership described by "mission command" brings to the fore the problem that very different missions and quickly changing circumstances on the ground make it practically less and less possible to steer individual actions within military missions by way of a central command. This problem is compounded by the fact that contemporary missions make it difficult to prepare soldiers in advance, because they combine military combat readiness with soft goals, such as the establishment of trust in peace consolidation processes.

The situational flexibility that is generally necessary may be created through training with the help of simulations, but despite this it seems that deployment situations themselves are becoming more and more relevant as training experiences. This makes it difficult to subject the training and its actual effects to democratic control mechanisms. For that reason, according to Egnell, trust in individual soldiers replaces control:

> Therefore, most armed forces' doctrines on command and control emphasize the importance of *mission command* in complex environments, a philosophy of decentralized command based on trust and initiative. In essence, mission command involves giving orders about what to do and what the aims are, but not how to do it ... Thus, commanders are allowed to hold a "loose rein", allowing subordinates freedom of action, while at the same time requiring them to exercise initiative and adjust actions according to new inputs of information. This means that commanders make fewer

decisions, but it allows them to focus on the most important ones … There is, however, always an element of increased risk involved in mission command, the risk that the subordinates have not really understood the intent, or the risk that the commander has made a bad decision or provided too few resources. Mission command theory, therefore, always involves a trade-off between ineffective but safe command and effective but risky command. Dealing with such risk requires mutual trust between superiors and subordinates.[78]

The leadership concept of mission command increases the responsibility and accountability of military subordinates, and likewise that of military leaders. Moreover, the professional position of military subordinates as responsible actors within a network of political and multinational military-to-military and civil-military relations requires a very high level of qualifications, which can no longer be derived from a purely military training agenda. They include *inter alia* communication skills, management techniques and the ability to interact with subordinates on the basis of mutual understanding, as well as trust and goal-oriented assessment of those subordinates' capabilities. Such comprehensive training is not offered in all the countries studied. In this respect, a clear rift can be seen between the more affluent Western states and the post-socialist countries. In the post-socialist countries, efforts are visible to complement military education with the requisite civilian components. However, soldiers in Germany, Switzerland and the UK are clearly privileged in terms of the proportion and scope of the education they are offered: for example, seminars of a very high quality on management, decision training and coping with dilemmas are provided in these countries.

Contemporary concepts of military leadership stressing the individual soldiers' capacities to judge autonomously and think laterally are in practice also influenced by the degree to which the organizational culture of a country's military was influenced by such concepts in the past, or instead insisted on clear hierarchies and centralized command. In this regard, the extent of change and difficulty with adaptation to these new requirements are influenced by the maturity of the democratic system: the younger democracies of our sample have in general much greater difficulties in adapting to the norms of decentralized leadership and the idea of individual soldiers as stakeholders in the democratic system.

One further practical obstacle to reaching the new military leadership ideal lies in the known social selection effects of the reformed recruitment systems. Societal value changes have produced a widespread attitude of avoidance towards military service among the general population, and yet the military offers particularly attractive career options for those who are otherwise at a disadvantage in the labour market. Countries with established volunteer armies – such as the United States, United Kingdom or France – show signs of a growing social and educational rift between the class of political decision-makers and the members of the armed forces. While all-volunteer armies promise to solve the problem of avoidance of the military service obligation, they also create new challenges:

> The greater reliance on market forces for the mobilization of people for military service brings problems in its train ... Even though "leaner and meaner forces" are the dominant trend, the military continues to face a range of social, cultural, and demographic difficulties in recruiting enough people to meets its demands. This means that the military cannot rely on a flow of volunteers but has to proactively recruit and to design ever more imaginative attempts to attract people using a variety of financial and other incentives ... Meanwhile, especially in states with all-volunteer forces, the public becomes more distant from its military.[79]

The fact that an all-volunteer military tends to be even less representative of society than a conscription system, which only recruits a small part of a particular age cohort, thus creates the normative dilemma that equal burden sharing in defence of the polity is suspended. Moreover, the social selection effects that result create the practical problem that the military tends to lose the contest to recruit highly competent personnel, who are so much more needed today in sufficient numbers.[80]

CONCLUSIONS

The end of the bipolar world order brought about a crisis for established state defence institutions, not only (but most visibly) in Europe. This discussion has described how these changes in post-Cold War security concepts led to changes in security sector governance and in particular the role of the military. Post-socialist states faced the reinvention of their entire architecture of security sector governance on the basis of these new visions of security, threat and the relationship between the state and the citizenry. At the same time, Western European democracies were reinventing the roles of their militaries in the context of a new international security environment, broader and deeper European integration, and a new rationale for NATO. At a time of great change, democracies, both new and consolidated, lacked models of democratic control of the armed forces to which to aspire.

These changes were neither foreseen nor explained adequately by conventional civil-military relations theory. No one model of democratic civilian control exists, and each European democracy has developed its own resolution to the dilemma of integrating the military's use of violence into a democratic system based on different institutional and organizational arrangements. Yet beyond the focus on institutional aspects, and in particular how to make the role of the military compatible with democracy, civil-military relations offers no account of the integration of normative and social aspects of the military's role in democracy.

Democratic peace theory provides an alternative explanatory framework for the influence of a normative model of military-society relations in democracies. Based on Kant's vision of the democratic soldier within a volunteer militia army, the idea of the democratic soldier sharing a burden of care and responsibility with the population provides a mechanism to reconcile the capacity for lethal military force with a democratic framework that prioritizes non-violent conflict resolution. Yet the idealized nature of this normative model and the changes in national defence and military institutions since the end of the Cold War challenge this conception: at once conventional concepts of national defence have been challenged, while professionalization and rationalization have reinvented military institutions. These trends generate the question of how normative models of the military's place in society have responded to these changes: the soldier thus asks to what extent, if any, are Europe's militaries still influenced by the normative model of the democratic soldier?

The preceding section introduced the findings of the 12-case comparative study of post-socialist, traditional and consolidated democracies in Europe, explaining how changes in the normative model of democratic soldiering interact with the new roles and missions of the military. The trend away from conscript forces to professional, volunteer militaries was clear in all cases. Within the context of new domestic and international conditions, the irrelevance of military missions to immediate national security has changed the traditional rationale for maintaining the military: in short, something that was once genuinely the defence institution of a nation-state has been developing into a multifunctional organization that is expected to be capable of performing a panoply of tasks for security provision in a rather wide sense. Thus in all the cases studied, the image of a highly trained and specialized professional has replaced the former ideal of the patriotic warrior at the level of official discourse.

Comparative analysis further showed that whether a democracy decides on a volunteer or a conscript army, or some combination of the two, is a matter determined by the historical and political conditions dominant in each case. Nevertheless, arguments for increased efficiency and smaller, more flexible forces capable of a greater range of tasks in a more complex technical environment do work in favour of military professionalization, minimizing arguments for democratic integration of the military through conscription.

The overarching trend towards professionalization and the growing international and transnational influences on military institutions raised the question of whether European democracies continue to vary in their models of democratic control. The results of the comparative analysis show that the countries studied still express particular features, values and traditions specific to their own national contexts in their normative conceptualizations of the soldier. Thus in spite of the overall observable trend towards all-volunteer forces, democratic states still deal in different ways with the fundamental issue of balancing democratic containment of the military with its operational capabilities. Although democracies continue to vary in their specific responses to the challenges of integrating the military into society, the centre of variance has shifted from recruitment systems to other aspects, such as democratic control (especially over troop deployment), the legitimization of military missions and their scope, and the rights, duties and missions assigned to military personnel.

This continuity in the existing normative models for soldiers creates a contradiction with the new concepts of soldiering that have been overlaid in the countries studied as a result of post-Cold War defence transformations. The analysis shows that while post-modern concepts of global values and collective security may serve to legitimize military missions at the official level, within the military itself the conventional image of national defender and patriot often remains more powerful. The consequence of this mismatch in normative models is that it may become increasingly difficult to reconcile the motivations and self-image of military personnel with their missions and role in the new democratic orders.

In concrete terms, the military transformation and the misfit between old and new normative models of soldiering pose challenges for military training and education in general, and military leadership. While old conceptions of soldiering focused on the trained conscript as national defender, the new vision of the soldier combines civilian and military tasks in the profile of a highly trained specialist professional. Moreover, the new mission types in which the military now engages require a new concept of leadership based on decentralized command. The shift away from central command towards individual decision-making and lateral thinking has posed challenges in all cases, but has been especially keenly felt in the post-socialist states.

One conclusion that may be drawn from this analysis of the new constellations of democratic civil-military relations is that the military should, in its own interest, insist on (more) scrupulous democratic control of the collective means of force, and on clear criteria concerning deployments:

> Rather than being the beast which must be contained in its institutional cage, it is the military that must have the greatest interest in being controlled in a truly democratic way, because this is probably its best chance to escape reckless, ill-advised, high-risk, overly costly and unnecessary operations.[81]

In democratic systems, soldiers are entitled to the assurance that they are deployed for sound reason, not least in order to be able to cope with the personal risks involved. Ultimately, democratic constituencies are accountable for engaging their collective means of violence, yet the retrenchment of sovereignty, in the context of the post-Cold War internationalization of security policy, has challenged this paradigm. How can, and how should, legitimacy, responsibility, control and accountability be organized when soldiers are supposed to be acting less on behalf of their national sovereign and increasingly as the guardians of the order of a transnational (be it European or world) value community? Military missions of this transnational kind may increase further, be it within the context of NATO or under the EU Common Foreign and Security Policy, but democratic control is as yet precariously organized in security communities where decisions are negotiated without involving national parliaments.[82] It is all the more important to watch whether democracies that deploy military forces under conditions of internationalization succeed in controlling their operations in such a way that the emphasis remains on civilizing conflicts. A deficit in the transparency and accountability of political decisions makes effective democratic control difficult in the same way as do imprecise defence policy guidelines.

In practical terms, the members of the armed forces have to redefine their professional identities and adjust to the new demands which unfold in the gap between the norms of national defence and the ambiguous realities of international missions, even if this very gap is hardly made an issue in the public representation of contemporary military missions. Scholars in the subject of democratic civil-military relations agree that comprehensive democratic control includes public attention and reflection; but that seems to be missing in many countries even at the level of the representatives of constituencies in parliaments and oversight bodies. Our comparative research has shown that the so-called "second generation problematic",[83] i.e. the effective engagement of civil society in the democratic governance of the defence and security sector, is not only a problem of the relatively young post-socialist democracies but symptomatic of a more general deficit, albeit for different reasons. It is important to consider that it is the mechanisms of democratic control that are actually practised which reduce the inclinations of democratic states to intervene with military means.[84] Such restraints can disappear if the opportunities for public involvement and/or the interest of the political public in exercising their rights of control diminish. Regrettably, our study shows this to be the case in a number of countries. The changes in recruitment systems are not only a consequence but also a cause of this trend, because bonding effects that were once formed through conscription have been lost. This has placed extra strain on the mutual democratic responsibilities of civil society, political leadership and military organizations in the transition to an all-volunteer army.

The effects of this disconnect between the military, the political sphere and society are reflected in the fact that many soldiers interviewed felt abandoned in the face of the fundamental challenges they were encountering. Our military interlocutors were experiencing simultaneous transformations in the international system and the defence alliance, in life-worlds, recruitment systems, military technology, mission types and – in the post-socialist countries – also the political system. All this implies a loss of orientation marks such as tradition, clear enemies, role certainties, identities and bonds with "parent societies", which may have been taken for granted.[85] The net result of these transformations is an enhanced complexity that needs to be tackled by the armed forces and their members alike.

Across the countries studied, the normative hybridization of professional conceptions of the soldier is a common response to the new ambiguities which arise from stretched understandings of national security, contingent deployments and blurred civil-military task profiles. The composites that can be found in official documents thus reflect changes in current norms of soldiering. The convergent image of the professional soldier as a multipurpose expert has not, however, replaced the nationally

     Sabine Mannitz

specific accentuations of traditional soldier concepts, which stress the emotional bonds with the nation and/or polity rather than loyalty *vis-à-vis* an imagined global value community. The new profile of soldiering has in many cases entered the normative discourse in the shape of an additional layer that partly merges and partly competes with the older concepts. The contradictions are most visible where the conditionalities associated with NATO or EU terms of integration were met by a sheer integration of templates and text blocks into the previous national conceptualizations.

This dilemma of competing expectations that draw the military in different directions is reflected, too, by a great number of the affected soldiers. Many of them, at different ranks and throughout almost all the countries in our sample, either observed alienation processes or expressed fears of that sort on both levels of domestic relations: towards the politicians who decide on troop deployments under pressure from the international community, and towards the democratic citizenries that are in charge of controlling this decision-making through parliament and the media, but seem to lose interest the more distant the actual military missions become from home defence purposes. Hence although we found overwhelming consent among soldiers in favour of the ongoing trend of transformations towards more professionalized, all-volunteer forces that may be tasked with complex missions, there is also widespread concern that politicians and the civilian public could come to regard the military as just a functional institution and thereby lower their inhibitions concerning deployment decisions.

Although the findings of this study are limited in their immediate applicability to the European context, it is clear that the increasing internationalization of military operations raises questions beyond Europe and beyond the functional level concerning the compatibility of troop modules, security policy strategies and military doctrines. What is not clear yet is what these developments lead to. If the conceptual elimination of national boundaries with regard to security is to be understood in the future as the obligation to intervene – as the norm of the "responsibility to protect" suggests, which has after all been accepted by the United Nations – this means fundamental changes for democratic civil-military relations and for the conceptualization of the soldier. Apart from the already observable trend of an increased merging of civilian with military role-sets in the troops' task allocations, seemingly "unmilitary" operations are mostly justified with the help of appeals to values which are generally respected in democratic social orders. However, it will have further consequences for national sovereignty, for political accountability, for the skills profiles of soldiers and – not least – for the balance between civilians and the military if the armed forces take on more and more such tasks with international mandates. The shift requires particular attention in view of fears that with the suspension of conscription and the availability of efficient professionalized armed forces, democratic states could more often and more easily approve use of military force as an instrument to pursue their political ends.

NOTES

[1]   The author wishes to thank Fairlie Chappuis, Heiner Hänggi, Albrecht Schnabel and the anonymous reviewers for their helpful comments.

[2]   Christopher Daase, "Wandel der Sicherheitskultur", *Aus Politik und Zeitgeschichte*, 50, 2010, pp. 9–16. See also Albrecht Schnabel and Marc Krupanski, "Mapping Evolving Internal Roles of the Armed Forces", SSR Paper 7, DCAF, Geneva, 2012.

[3]   For the purpose of this paper, the security sector is understood in the narrow, state-centred meaning as consisting of those state institutions which are given the formal mandate and the means to protect the polity with the use of force, and those state institutions which control and oversee them. Broader concepts of the security sector, such as that adopted by UNDP, *Human Development Report* (Oxford: Oxford University Press, 2002), point to the fact that sustainable security governance, in particular in post-conflict reconstruction settings, affects many more societal and political factors than the aforementioned state institutions (on the shift towards people-centred security definitions, see further Ursula C. Schroeder, "Measuring Security Sector Governance – A Guide to Relevant Indicators", Occasional Paper 20, DCAF, Geneva, 2010). Given the focus of the present research on military reforms across Europe, a narrower definition of the security sector was more appropriate. Nevertheless, the role of non-state institutions, including e.g. the powerful Lithuanian Riflemen's Association, was considered in our case studies wherever country experts considered them to be a significant part of the national landscape of security governance and an expression of a particular security culture.

[4]   There is no single authoritative definition of SSR but there is a remarkable convergence in major policy statements, e.g. of the EU, African Union, OECD and UN as well as major bilateral donors. The OECD played a major role in the 1990s and early years of this millennium in conceptualizing SSR as attempts to transform the security system – inclusive of all actors involved in security governance – in order to improve the degree to which the system functions in accordance with principles of democracy and good governance: OECD, *Security System Reform and Governance* (Paris: OECD, 2004). Today, the UN is playing the lead role and SSR is regarded as a core element of UN peacekeeping and peacebuilding efforts. In 2007 the Inter-Agency Security Sector Reform Task Force was created, followed by the establishment of a special SSR unit to serve as an institutional focal point and provide resource capacity. These efforts aim to develop and promote an integrated and multidimensional approach. The United Nations refers to SSR as "a process of assessment, review and implementation as well as monitoring and evaluation led by national authorities that has as its goal the enhancement of effective and accountable security for the State and its peoples without discrimination and with full respect for human rights and the rule of law": UN Department of Peacekeeping Operations, Office of Rule of Law and Security Institutions, Security Sector Reform Unit, *The United Nations SSR Perspective* (New York: United Nations, 2012, p. 2). For an introduction to the background and development of the SSR concept see, for instance, Theodor Winkler, "Managing Change: The Reform and Democratic Control of the Security Sector and International Order", Occasional Paper 1, DCAF, Geneva, 2002; Alan Bryden and Philipp Fluri, *Security Sector Reform: Institutions, Society and Good Governance* (Baden-Baden: Nomos, 2003); Andrzej Karkoszka, "The

Concept of Security Sector Reform", in *Security Sector Reform: Its Relevance for Conflict Prevention, Peace Building, and Development* (Geneva: UN Office at Geneva, 2003, pp. 9–15); Alan Bryden and Heiner Hänggi (eds), *Reform and Reconstruction of the Security Sector* (Münster: LIT Verlag, 2004); Christoph Bleiker and Marc Krupanski, "The Rule of Law and Security Sector Reform: Conceptualising a Complex Relationship", SSR Paper 5, DCAF, Geneva, 2012.

[5]　Ulrich Schneckener, "Post-Westfalia trifft Prä-Westfalia", in Egbert Jahn, Sabine Fischer and Astrid Sahm (eds), *Die Zukunft des Friedens* (Wiesbaden: VS Verlag für Sozialwissenschaften, 2005, pp. 189–211); Wulf Herbert, "Security Sector Reform in Developing and Transitional Countries Revisited", in Beatrix Austin, Martina Fischer and Hans J. Giessmann (eds), *Advancing Conflict Transformation. Berghof Handbook II* (Leverkusen: Barbara Budrich Publishers, 2011), www.berghof-handbook.net.

[6]　On "securitization" see Barry Buzan, Ole Waever and Jaap de Wilde, *Security: A New Framework for Analysis* (Boulder, CO: Lynne Rienner, 1998); and in the particular context of security sector organs see Heiner Hänggi, "Making Sense of Security Sector Governance", in Heiner Hänggi and Theodor Winkler (eds), *Challenges of Security Sector Governance* (Münster: LIT Verlag, 2003, pp. 1–21).

[7]　Immanuel Kant, "Zum Ewigen Frieden. Ein philosophischer Entwurf", in Wilhelm Weischedel (ed.), *Werkausgabe Band XI* (Frankfurt: Suhrkamp Verlag, 1997, pp. 195–251).

[8]　The empirical findings, however, state that democracies are no less inclined to wage war than non-democracies, but they do not fight against other democracies. See Anna Geis, "Diagnose: Doppelbefund – Ursache: ungeklärt? Die Kontroversen um den 'demokratischen Frieden'", *Politische Vierteljahresschrift*, 42(2), 2001, pp. 282–298.

[9]　Ruth Seifert, "Soldatische Subjektivität, gesellschaftlicher Wandel und Führungsanforderungen", Working Paper 69, SOWI, Munich, 1992; Ruth Seifert, "Individualisierungsprozesse, Geschlechterverhältnisse und die soziale Konstruktion des Soldaten", Berichte 61, SOWI, Munich, 1993.

[10]　Besides Ruth Seifert (see note 9), others raised this argument as well: Wilfried von Bredow, "Entgrenzung militärischer Organisationen? Militarisierung der Gesellschaft versus Zivilisierung der Streitkräfte", in Wolfgang Vogt (ed.), *Militär als Gegenkultur? Streitkräfte im Wandel der Gesellschaft* (Opladen: Leske + Budrich, 1986); Wilfried von Bredow, "Erkundungsziel: 'Militärwelt'. Vorüberlegungen zu einer ethnomethodologischen Erweiterung der Militärsoziologie", in Wolfgang Vogt (ed.), *Militär als Lebenswelt. Streitkräfte im Wandel der Gesellschaft Bd. 2* (Opladen: Leske + Budrich, 1988, p. 177); Laura Miller, "Feminism and the Exclusion of Army Women from Combat", *Gender Issues*, 16(3), 1998, pp. 33–64; Paul Klein, "Menschenführung – Aufgabe und Erfüllung", in Anton Steer (ed.), *Menschen führen im Heer* (Frankfurt: Report Verlag, 1989); Ekkehard Lippert, "Die gegenwärtige Lage der Militärsoziologie", SOWI, Munich, 1992; Gerhard Kümmel, "Die Feminisierung der Streitkräfte", in Karl W. Haltiner and Paul Klein (eds), *Europas Armeen im Umbruch* (Baden-Baden: Nomos, 2002); Klaus Naumann, *Generale in der Demokratie. Generationsgeschichtliche Studien zur Bundeswehrelite* (Hamburg: Hamburger Edition, 2007).

[11]　Military sociology has been studying the military as a social institution for many decades, but has largely neglected questions of how institutional regulations and social practices in society and the military relate to one another, and what kind of cognitive interactions are

involved. On the desiderata of research on the military in democracy see Alexander L. George and Andrew Bennett, "Case Study Methods and Research on the Interdemocratic Peace", in Alexander L. George and Andrew Bennett (eds), *Case Studies and Theory Development in the Social Sciences* (Cambridge, MA: MIT Press, 2005, pp. 45–58). Cf. Miriam F. Elman, *Paths to Peace. Is Democracy the Answer?* (Cambridge, MA: MIT Press, 1997, p. 33); Tarak Barkawi and Mark Laffey, "Introduction", in Tarak Barkawi and Mark Laffey (eds), *Democracy, Liberalism, and War: Rethinking the Democratic Peace Debate* (Boulder, CO: Lynne Rienner, 2001); Raymond Duvall and Jutta Weldes, "The International Relations of Democracy, Liberalism, and War", in Tarak Barkawi and Mark Laffey (eds), *Democracy, Liberalism, and War: Rethinking the Democratic Peace Debate* (Boulder, CO: Lynne Rienner, 2001).

[12] Ulrich Hundt, "Das Bild vom modernen Soldaten. Erziehung und innere Führung", *Loyal*, 9, 1992, p. 5.

[13] We owe great thanks to the Volkswagen Foundation, Hannover, for funding the international research on "The Image of the Democratic Soldier in European Comparison" from 2006 to 2010. For more on the individual cases see www.hsfk.de/The-Image-of-the-Democratic-Soldier-Tensions-betw.75.0.html?&L=1 and Sabine Mannitz (ed.), *Democratic Civil-Military Relations. Soldiering in 21st Century Europe* (London: Routledge, 2012).

[14] Harald Müller, Marco Fey, Sabine Mannitz and Niklas Schörnig, "Democracy, the Armed Forces and Military Deployment: The 'Second Social Contract' Is on the Line", Report No. 108, PRIF, Frankfurt, 2011, p. 10.

[15] See Anthony Forster and William Wallace, "What Is NATO For?", *Survival*, 43(4), 2001, pp. 107–122.

[16] Karl W. Haltiner and Jonathan Bennett, "GsoA-Initiativen 1989 und 2001 – Das gewandelte Bild der Miliz in der Bevölkerung", *Allgemeine Schweizerische Militärzeitung*, 5, 2002, pp. 21–24.

[17] See Anthony Forster, *Armed Forces and Society in Europe* (Basingstoke: Palgrave Macmillan, 2006, pp. 1–4).

[18] Ibid., p. 2.

[19] Karl Haltiner and Paul Klein, "The European Post-Cold War Military Reforms and Their Impact on Civil-Military Relations", in Franz Kernic, Paul Klein and Karl Haltiner (eds), *The European Armed Forces in Transition* (Frankfurt: Peter Lang, 2005, pp. 9–30).

[20] This distinction is a synthesized summary from ibid., pp. 9–19.

[21] Forster, note 17 above, p. 4.

[22] See Matthias Dembinski, "Von der kollektiven Verteidigung in Europa zur weltweiten Intervention? Das neue strategische Konzept der Kosovo-Krieg und die Zukunft der NATO", Standpunkte No. 3, HSFK, Frankfurt, 1999; Forster, note 17 above, pp. 152–167.

[23] See Anthony Forster and William Wallace, "Common Foreign and Security Policy: A New Policy or Just a New Name?", in Helen Wallace and William Wallace (eds), *Policy Making in the European Union*, 4th edn (Oxford: Oxford University Press, 2000, pp. 411–435).

[24] Haltiner and Klein, note 19 above, p. 11.

[25] Forster, note 17 above, p. 20.

[26] In structural terms, the special feature of a democracy's internal relationship with its military is the fact that civil control of the military power apparatus takes place under the decision-making primacy of the democratically legitimated political leadership. This is the standard

principle of democratic governance, and is indispensable for states which are undergoing the process of democratization. See Manfred G. Schmidt, *Demokratietheorien* (Opladen: Leske + Budrich, 2000), pp. 450ff. Corresponding institutional reforms took place during the wave of democratization in post-socialist Europe, but since there were hardly any civilian experts in military issues available outside Communist Party circles, it was problematic to fill the structure with life and make sure that democratic control was executed effectively.

[27] On the level of the structural changes in the military constitutions, levels of military participation and changed recruitment principles, the reforms are well researched. See, for example, Karl Haltiner and Paul Klein (eds), *Europas Armeen in Umbruch* (Baden-Baden: Nomos, 2002); Ines-Jacqueline Werkner, "Allgemeine Trends und Entwicklungslinien in den europäischen Wehrsystemen", SOWI Working Paper 134, Sozialwissenschaftliches Institut der Bundeswehr, Strausberg, 2003; Tibor Szvircsev Tresch, "Europas Streitkräfte im Wandel: Von der Wehrpflichtarmee zur Freiwilligenstreitkraft. Eine empirische Untersuchung europäischer Streitkräfte 1975 bis 2003", doctoral dissertation, University of Zurich, 2005, www.google.ch/url?sa=t&rct=j&q=&esrc=s&source=web&cd=2&ved=0CDkQFjAB&url=http%3A%2F%2Fmercury.ethz.ch%2Fserviceengine%2FFiles%2FISN%2F13572%2Fipublicationdocument_singledocument%2F5f4ed3d6-cb24-4324-ade6-5e89f80ff e96%2Fde%2FDissertation%2BSzvircsev.pdf&ei=akRRUuf0JorWtAbNmIBo&usg=AFQjCNGZD3ZJHzS4u0fDzenBQO26Vqow3w&bvm=bv.53537100,d.Yms.

[28] Benedict Anderson, *Imagined Communities: Reflections on the Origin and Spread of Nationalism* (London: Verso, 1991).

[29] See Niklas Schörnig, "Opfersensibilität und Friedensdividende. Legitimationsmuster einer aktiven amerikanischen Rüstungsindustriepolitik in den 1990er Jahren", *Zeitschrift für Internationale Beziehungen*, 14(1), 2007, pp. 9–42; Niklas Schörnig, "Visionen unblutiger Kriege", in Anna Geis, Harald Müller and Wolfgang Wagner (eds), *Schattenseiten des Demokratischen Friedens* (Frankfurt: Campus, 2007); Niklas Schörnig, "Macht und Opfervermeidung", in Jan Helmig and Niklas Schörnig (eds), *Die Transformation der Streitkräfte im 21. Jahrhundert* (Frankfurt: Campus, 2008); Niklas Schörnig, "Casualty Aversion in Democratic Security Provision: Procurement and the Defence Industrial Base", in Matthew Evangelista, Harald Müller and Niklas Schörnig (eds), *Democracy and Security. Preferences, Norms and Policy-making* (London: Routledge, 2008); Niklas Schörnig, "In der Opferfalle", Standpunkte No. 2, HSFK, Frankfurt, 2009; Bernard Boëne, "How 'Unique' Should The Military Be?", *Archives Européennes de Sociologie*, 31(1), 1990, pp. 3–59; Lawrence Freedman, *The Revolution in Strategic Affairs*, Adelphi Papers No. 318 (Oxford: Oxford University Press for International Institute for Strategic Studies, 1998); Christopher Dandeker, "On the Need to Be Different: Recent Trends in Military Culture", in Hew Strachan (ed.), *The British Army: Manpower and Society into the Twenty-first Century* (London: Frank Cass, 2000).

[30] See Sabine Mannitz, "Placed in a Modern Dilemma: Democratic Militaries in the Struggle of Role Reinvention", *Zeitschrift für Ethnologie*, 131(2), 2006, pp. 301–323.

[31] Samuel A. Stouffer, Edward A. Suchman, Leland C. DeVinney, Shirley A. Star and Robin M. Williams Jr, *Studies in Social Psychology in World War II: The American Soldier,* 4 vols (Princeton, NJ: Princeton University Press, 1949).

[32] This was also the starting point of the renowned Inter-University Seminar on Armed Forces and Society and its refereed journal *Armed Forces & Society*.

[33] See Günther Wachtler (ed.), *Militär, Krieg, Gesellschaft. Texte zur Militärsoziologie* (Frankfurt: Campus, 1983, pp. 11ff).

[34] Ibid.

[35] Franz Kernic, "Entwicklungslinien der modernen Militärsoziologie", *Österreichische Militärische Zeitschrift*, 39(5), 2001, p. 573.

[36] Samuel P. Huntington, *The Soldier and the State: The Theory and Politics of Civil-Military Relations*, (Cambridge: Cambridge University Press, 1957); Morris Janowitz, *The Professional Soldier: A Social and Political Portrait* (New York: Free Press, [1960] 1971).

[37] Janowitz, ibid., p. xi.

[38] Peter D. Feaver, "The Civil-Military Problematique: Huntington, Janowitz, and the Question of Civilian Control", *Armed Forces & Society*, 23(2), 1996, p. 167.

[39] Rebecca Schiff's concordance model is such an exceptional work: Rebecca Schiff, *The Military and Domestic Politics* (New York: Routledge, 2009). She uses four indicators for her theory of concordance – social composition of the officer corps, recruitment method, military style and the political decision-making process – to argue that the military, political elites and the citizenry are to agree upon the interconnections of these indicators in order to establish a functioning relationship. Her studies take political culture seriously, and point to the impact of democratic deliberation processes in the search for consensual solutions.

[40] Feaver, note 38 above.

[41] Pascal Vennesson, "Civil-Military Relations in France. Is There a Gap?", *Journal of Strategic Studies*, 26(2), 2003, p. 33.

[42] For more on this point see Hew Strachan, "The Civil-Military 'Gap' in Britain", *Journal of Strategic Studies*, 26(2), 2003, pp. 43–63; James Burk, "Theories of Democratic Civil-Military Relations", *Armed Forces & Society*, 29(1), 2002, pp. 7–29. Parallel to this thread of the debate, there was an argument in the Federal Republic of Germany from the late 1960s onwards at the point where military sociology meets peace research. It dealt with the rationality and moral impacts of a security policy based on nuclear weapons, and shifted to the societal integration of the Bundeswehr in the 1980s. When the Cold War came to an end, and with it (or so it seemed) the danger of a nuclear war, the debate associated with the "theorem of incompatibility" petered out. On the rationality and moral impacts of a security policy see for example Ralf Zoll (ed.), *Wie integriert ist die Bundeswehr? Zum Verhältnis von Militär und Gesellschaft in der Bundesrepublik* (Munich: Piper, 1979); Ralf Zoll, *Sicherheit und Militär: Genese, Struktur und Wandel von Meinungsbildern in Militär und Gesellschaft; Ergebnisse und Analyseansätze im internationalen Vergleich* (Opladen: Westdeutscher Verlag, 1982); Karl Hegner, Ekkehard Lippert and Roland Wakenhut, *Selektion oder Sozialisation: Zur Entwicklung des politischen und moralischen Bewußtseins in der Bundeswehr* (Opladen: Westdeutscher Verlag, 1983). On the "theorem of incompatibility" see Wolfgang R. Vogt (ed.), *Sicherheitspolitik und Streitkräfte in der Legitimitätskrise. Analysen zum Prozess der Delegitimierung des Militärischen im Kernwaffenzeitalter* (Baden-Baden: Nomos, 1983); Wolfgang Vogt (ed.), *Militär als Gegenkultur? Streitkräfte im Wandel der Gesellschaft* (Opladen: Leske + Budrich, 1986).

[43] See further Hänggi, note 6 above.

[44] See, for instance, Berthold Meyer, "Von der Entscheidungsmündigkeit zur Entscheidungsmüdigkeit? Nach zehn Jahren Parlamentsvorbehalt für Bundeswehreinsätze naht ein Beteiligungsgesetz", Report 4, HSFK, Frankfurt, 2004.

[45] This is the argument of Andrew Cottey, Timothy Edmunds and Anthony Foster (eds), *The Challenge of Military Reform in Postcommunist Europe: Building Professional Armed Forces* (Basingstoke: Palgrave Macmillan, 2002, p. 36).

[46] See also Burk, note 42 above.

[47] E.g. Jeffrey Simon, *NATO and the Czech and Slovak Republics: A Comparative Study in Civil-Military Relations* (Lanham, MD: Rowman & Littlefield, 2004).

[48] E.g. Anthony Forster, *New Civil-Military Relations and Its Research Agendas* (Geneva: DCAF, 2002); Marina Caparini, *Lessons Learned and Upcoming Research Issues in Democratic Control of Armed Forces and Security Sector Reform* (Geneva: DCAF, 2002); Hans Born, Marina Caparini and Karl W. Haltiner, *Models of Democratic Control of the Armed Forces: A Multi-Country Study Comparing "Good Practices" of Democratic Control* (Geneva: DCAF, 2002).

[49] One must mention the exceptional research project on "The Transformation of Civil-Military Relations in Comparative Context" conducted within the framework of the ESRC programme *One Europe or Several?*. It has looked at post-socialist states and the reforms introduced as they have reorganized their civil-military relations since 1989/1990. See Andrew Cottey, Timothy Edmunds and Anthony Foster (eds), *Democratic Control of the Military in Postcommunist Europe: Guarding the Guards* (Basingstoke: Palgrave Macmillan, 2001); Cottey et al., note 45 above; Andrew Cottey, Timothy Edmunds and Anthony Foster (eds), *Soldiers and Societies in Postcommunist Europe: Legitimacy and Change* (Basingstoke: Palgrave Macmillan, 2003).

[50] Kant, note 7 above, pp. 197–198.

[51] See Harald Müller and Jonas Wolff, "Democratic Peace: Many Data, Little Explanation?", in Anna Geis, Lothar Brock and Harald Müller (eds), *Democratic Wars. Looking at the Dark Side of Democratic Peace* (Basingstoke: Palgrave Macmillan, 2006); Anna Geis, Harald Müller and Niklas Schörnig (eds), *The Janus Face of Liberal Democracies: Militant "Forces for Good"* (Cambridge: Cambridge University Press, 2013).

[52] Bruce Russett and John Oneal, *Triangulating Peace: Democracy, Interdependence, and International Organizations* (New York: W. W. Norton, 2001); Matthias Dembinski and Andreas Hasenclever (eds), *Die internationale Organisation des Demokratischen Friedens. Studien zur Leistungsfähigkeit regionaler Sicherheitsinstitutionen* (Baden-Baden: Nomos, 2010).

[53] Georg Nolte and Heike Krieger, *Europäische Wehrrechtssysteme. Ein Vergleich der Rechtsordnungen Belgiens, Dänemarks, Deutschlands, Frankreichs, Luxemburgs, der Niederlande, Polens, Spaniens und des Vereinigten Königreichs*, Forum Innere Führung Vol. 17 (Baden-Baden: Nomos, 2002, p. 20; see also pp. 34–39, 72–77); Dirk Peters, Wolfgang Wagner and Nicole Deitelhoff, "The Parliamentary Control of European Security Policy", RECON Report 3/2008, ARENA-Centre for European Studies, Oslo, 2008.

[54] As mentioned, the phases of democratization make up just one criterion for the selection of cases that cannot be discussed in full here for reasons of limited space. Some important characteristics of the selected country cases are compiled in Table 2.

[55] Methodologically, to supplement the analysis of written material and the contents of training and education, the research team conducted non-participant observations in military academies where possible and semi-structured interviews with soldiers (mostly NCOs and officer ranks) in all cases. It was not possible in all the sample countries to obtain

the necessary Ministry of Defence permits for conducting fieldwork in military institutions, but all researchers found ways at least to conduct the interviews. This research phase provided rich information about the habitual routines and subjective attitudes that soldiers had developed in the different countries. Several markers were used to characterize differences in this regard, making use of hypotheses derived from democratic peace theory. To give one example, we had anticipated that soldiers from different democracies develop a connected variance in the complexity of their self-images and their images of "the other" and "the enemy", so that in countries where the values of the Enlightenment are incorporated extensively in training – e.g. by giving humanitarian law a prominent place in instruction – the aforementioned categorizations could be expected to be expressed in the most differentiated terms. With the help of such theoretically grounded markers, reconstructive typologies were drawn up of the concepts that soldiers expressed in the interviews; and these were ultimately assessed with reference to the official norms of the respective country.

[56] For an overview of the changes in recruitment systems see Werkner, note 27 above; Tresch, note 27 above.

[57] Charles C. Moskos, "Towards a Postmodern Military: The United States as Paradigm", in Charles C. Moskos, John A. Williams and David R. Segal (eds), *The Postmodern Military* (Oxford: Oxford University Press, 2000, p. 15); see also Owen Cote, "The Personal Needs of the Future Force", in Cindy Williams (ed.), *Filling the Ranks* (Cambridge, MA: MIT Press, 2004); Werkner, note 27 above.

[58] See Müller et al., note 14 above, p. 1.

[59] Heiner Hänggi, "Conceptualizing Security Sector Reform and Reconstruction", in Bryden and Hänggi, note 4 above, pp. 4–5.

[60] See Müller et al., note 14 above, p. 1.

[61] The distinction between "wars of necessity" and "wars of choice" was used by Richard Haass in his political memoirs of the two Iraq wars. Haass was a member of the National Security Council staff for the first President Bush and director of policy planning in the State Department for his son. He contrasts the two wars, and distinguishes the 1991 war as one of necessity and the 2003 invasion as one of choice. Richard N. Haass, *War of Necessity, War of Choice: A Memoir of Two Iraq Wars* (New York: Simon & Schuster, 2009).

[62] For details concerning the situation in Serbia see Filip Ejdus, "Democratic Security Sector Governance in Serbia", Report No. 94, PRIF, Frankfurt, 2010; Filip Ejdus, "State Building and the Image of the Democratic Soldier in Serbia", in Mannitz, note 13 above, pp. 226–248.

[63] All these particularities cannot be presented and discussed here. For the countries studied, detailed reports can be obtained at www.hsfk.de/Das-Bild-vom-demokratischen-Soldaten-Spannungen-z.75.0.html?&L=1 and from the joint publication of the research results (Mannitz, note 13 above).

[64] Samuel Huntington's idea of "objective control" has found much attention in this context. It is based on the volunteer soldier whose service under arms is not derived from his/her status as a citizen, but from a professional mission. See Huntington, note 36 above.

[65] This is one of the core theses employed by Kant in his democratic peace argument against standing armies. It lacks empirical verification as much as it lacks falsification thus far, for the tendency among democratic states to vocationalize their armed forces and contract out some functions to private companies is still a rather recent one. At Kant's time, the novelty

of the *levée en masse* marked the republican understanding of the citizenries' rights, including the right to carry weapons to defend the polity. Standing armies and mercenaries constituted the typical military infrastructure of the undemocratic rulers of the time.

[66] This variation filters the extent of possible control: if the executive branch of the political system has a greater degree of independence from the legislature and the mode of control is weaker, it is in a better position to take governmental decisions more swiftly. When this is a matter of concrete situations relating to the missions of the armed forces, it can place limitations on the participatory discourse – in other words, it is less likely that civil society will be able to influence the outcome. If, on the other hand, the executive has a clearer constitutional obligation to listen to the views of the legislature, there is a greater prospect that the population will be able to participate discursively. This also applies to other specific democratic institutions such as the freedom of the media and the executive's duty of transparency in relation to the legislature and public opinion. These democratic institutions make their own contribution to conditioning public discourses on the role and tasks of the armed forces. See also Miriam F. Elman, "Unpacking Democracy: Presidentialism, Parliamentarism, and Theories of Democratic Peace", *Security Studies*, 9(4), 2000, pp. 91–126.

[67] See Nolte and Krieger, note 53 above, pp. 72–77.

[68] Ilana Bet-El, "Media and Conflict: An Integral Part of the Modern Battlefield", in Michael Kobi, David Kellen and Eyal Ben-Ari (eds), *The Transformation of the World of War and Peace Support Operations* (Westport, CT: Praeger, 2009, p. 72).

[69] See Karl W. Haltiner and Gerhard Kümmel, "The Hybrid Soldier: Identity Changes in the Military", in Giuseppe Caforio, Christopher Dandeker and Gerhard Kümmel (eds), *Armed Forces, Soldiers, and Civil-Military Relations. Essays in Honor of Jürgen Kuhlmann* (Wiesbaden: VS Verlag, 2008).

[70] See Janowitz, note 36 above. The increasing extent of outsourcing of traditionally military tasks to civilian service providers is another aspect that mirrors the previous functional civilianization within the armed forces.

[71] Details on these and the other country cases are compiled in Mannitz, note 13 above.

[72] The cumulative stress for soldiers which results from simultaneous transformations of the political system, the defence alliance, the military structure, technology, life-worlds and missions is discussed in greater detail by Harald Müller, "Transformation Stress: Democratic Soldiers between Ideals and Mission Impossible", in Mannitz, note 13 above.

[73] See Moskos, note 57 above, for his concept of a "postmodern" military.

[74] These contradictions are spelled out in the country reports, www.hsfk.de/Das-Bild-vom-demokratischen-Soldaten-Spannungen-z.75.0.html?&L=1, and in Mannitz, note 13 above.

[75] The term was coined by Christopher Dandeker in view of the controversy surrounding the invasion of Iraq in the UK and other countries that had joined the "coalition of the willing". Christopher Dandeker, "Surveillance and Military Transformation: Organizational Trends in Twenty-first Century Armed Forces", in Kevin D. Haggerty and Richard V. Ericson (eds), *The New Politics of Surveillance and Visibility* (Toronto, ON: Toronto University Press, 2006).

[76] See, for instance, the following for an overview of themes and issues arising from the differentiation of military tasks: Christopher Dandeker, *Flexible Forces for the 21st Century* (Karlstadt: Swedish National Defence College, 1999); Volker Franke, *Preparing for Peace: Military Identity, Value Orientations, and Professional Military Education* (Westport, CT:

Praeger, 1999); Jean Callaghan and Mathias Schönborn (eds), *Warriors in Peacekeeping* (Münster: LIT Verlag, 2004); Karl W. Haltiner and Paul Klein, *Multinationalität als Herausforderung für die Streitkräfte* (Baden-Baden: Nomos, 2004).

[77] Christopher Dandeker, "The End of War? The Use of Force in the Twenty-first Century", in Michael Kobi, David Kellen and Eyal Ben-Ari (eds), *The Transformation of the World of War and Peace Support Operations* (Westport, CT: Praeger, 2009, p. 37).

[78] Robert Egnell, "Civil-Military Aspects of Effectiveness in Peace Support Operations", in Michael Kobi, David Kellen and Eyal Ben-Ari (eds), *The Transformation of the World of War and Peace Support Operations* (Westport, CT: Praeger, 2009, pp. 127–128).

[79] Dandeker, note 77 above, pp. 35–36.

[80] Marc Magee and Steven Nider, "Citizen Soldiers and the War on Terror", Policy Report, Progressive Policy Institute, Washington, DC, 17 December 2002.

[81] Müller, note 72 above.

[82] See Wolfgang Wagner, "The Democratic Control of Military Power Europe", *Journal of European Public Policy*, 13(2), 2006, pp. 200–216.

[83] Cottey et al., note 45 above.

[84] Todd S. Sechser, "Are Soldiers Less War-prone than Statesmen?", *Journal of Conflict Resolution*, 48(5), 2004, pp. 770ff.

[85] Guiseppe Caforio coined this expression for a conceptualization of the civil-military gap which he considers a functional necessity: Guiseppe Caforio (ed.), *Cultural Differences between the Military and Parent Society in Democratic Countries* (Amsterdam: Elsevier, 2007); see also Mannitz, note 30 above; Müller, note 72 above.